Managing information for research

Elizabeth Orna
with Graham Stevens

Open University Press
Buckingham • Philadelphia

Open University Press
Celtic Court
22 Ballmoor
Buckingham
MK18 1XW

and
1900 Frost Road
Suite 1001
Bristol
PA 19007
USA

First edition published 1995

A catalogue record of this book is
available from the British Library
ISBN 0 335 19398 6 (hb)
ISBN 0 335 19397 8 (pb)

**Library of Congress Cataloging-
in-Publication Data**
Orna, Elizabeth
  Managing information in research
  Elizabeth Orna with Graham Stevens
  p.   cm
Includes bibliographical references
  and index.
  ISBN−0 335−19398−6 (hb)
  ISBN−0 335−19397−8 (pb)
  1. Information resources management.
  2 Research. I. Stevens, Graham.
  II. Title.
  T58.64.O76 1995
  001.4--dc20
  95−13767 CIP

Typeset by Graham Stevens

Printed in Great Britain by Biddles
Limited, Guildford and King's Lynn

Contents

Preface

• 'Not being able to finish everything in time for deadlines.' • 'Going round in circles; losing perspective of what your aim is.' • 'Frustration at being unable to find "correct" information and resorting to an irrational research pattern – randomly choosing books and using the "luck" element. However in some cases this has proved rather successful – since areas of irrelevance have proved otherwise.'
(Students at the end of their first term of research, on problems they have experienced so far, and anxieties for the future).

Since the early 1980s, I have been privileged to work with students undertaking research in a variety of disciplines – most of them for the first time. My invitation to do so came from academic colleagues who knew that I specialized in writing and editing informative texts, and in 'doing things with information', and who felt that their students needed some help in that line.

I have learned a good deal in those ten years or so, most of it from the students themselves, who have been generous in sharing with me their experiences of research, and willing to trust my ideas enough to try some of them out. The outcomes have been encouraging enough to make me think it worthwhile to offer the ideas and the results of experience to a wider readership.

It seems particularly important to do so at the present time. Changes in higher education have brought more and more students into first-degree courses, and most of those courses now require some research for extended projects. But many students are finding that their previous educational experience has not prepared them either for handling the information that such projects require, or for writing about the results. More students than at any previous time are going on to research for higher degrees, but financial pressures in the system mean that they are thrown more on their own resources than has ever been the case before – often with little help in taking responsibility for their own learning. Other developments in higher education are putting increased emphasis on monitoring the progress and achievement of students, and that makes it important that they should be able to plan their work and monitor their own progress.

Apart from all that, it has never been easy to 'do research'. There are other underlying difficulties which exist regardless of the system, and seem to be related to how human beings think and feel. The main ones that I have observed, from my particular viewpoint, lie in:

- Making good use of information sources, and using time effectively in extracting information.
- Transforming information into structured internal knowledge.
- Managing the physical stores of information which researchers collect and create in the course of research, so that the content is accessible and usable.
- Scheduling the progress towards presenting the final written products of the research, and managing time throughout the period of the research.
- Integrating information collection with other research activities (for example, experimenting, testing, reflecting, discussion with peers and tutors).
- Transforming the knowledge acquired during the research into a final written product that is accessible to the intended users, and does justice to the work and the thinking that have gone into the research.
- Taking sole responsibility and being on one's own – the isolation of the researcher, and the anxiety which that can bring.

My observations seem to be borne out by the experience of students themselves. I have recently been asking groups of students to select the items from that list which cause them the most difficulty or anxiety; the ones most often mentioned are:

- Managing time
- Transforming knowledge into written form
- Organizing the information they collect
- Transforming information into internal knowledge
- Isolation and loss of confidence.

So I have concentrated on trying to provide both practical help, and some explanations of the nature of the difficulties, in the hope that readers will be able to relate them to their own experience, and draw on their own strengths in managing the difficult but sometimes exhilarating process of research.

I have one final reason for writing this book: after a gap of more years than I care to think of, I have recently embarked again on a research project, which I hope will in due course lead to a doctorate. It seems only fair to try what I recommend to readers on myself, and that is what I have done – most of the 'recipes' I suggest have been tried out at home.

Acknowledgements

My thanks are due to:
- Christina Arthurton for example material based on her research project.
- Simon Bell for permission to reproduce Figures 8.4 and 8.5, and for unfailing willingness to read and comment.
- Jim Bodoh for giving me the opportunity to consider the matters which form the subject of the book, and for allowing me to develop my ideas with his MA students.
- Ann Chasseaud for permission to quote from her MA thesis, and for perceptive comments.
- Jane Graves for permission to quote from an unpublished paper, and for many discussions about the problems that students face when they have to write seriously for the first time.
- Wolfgang Heidrich for example material based on his research.
- J. B. Hepworth and the *International Journal of Information Management* and Elsevier Science Limited for permission to reproduce Figure 8.7.
- Professor Emeritus P. K. M'Pherson for permission to reproduce Figure 8.8.
- Graham Stevens not only for writing the greater part of Chapter 9, but also for ingenious solutions to design problems involving the presentation of complex information, and creative interpretations of the illustrations.
- MA students in Graphics, Industrial Design and Textiles at Central St Martins College of Art and Design, Development Studies students at the University of East Anglia, and MSc Information Science students at City University, London – for completing the questionnaire referred to in the Preface.
- And finally, all the students with whom I have worked as a kind of 'dissertation coach', for being willing to try out some of my suggestions, and for all that I have learned from them.

1 | What are we doing when we 'do research'?

Research... , *sb* 1577. ...[1] *The act of searching (closely or carefully) for or after a specific thing or person.* [2] *An investigation directed to the discovery of some fact by careful study of a subject; a course of scientific inquiry.* Shorter Oxford Dictionary.

As dictionary definitions go, this is a reasonable one; it highlights the central stages of the activities that go under the name of research: *searching,* by means of *careful,* critical investigation, *in order to* discover *something* specific.

But if we make a diagrammatic representation of the processes as defined, it looks pretty thin (see Figure 1.1 on page 10). It's thin because it misses out other essential aspects of the process, in particular:

- What researchers do *before* the searching begins, in order to decide what they are looking for
- What they do *during* the searching, to ensure they can make good use of what they find
- What they do *after* their investigation has led to discovery, in order to communicate what they have found.

And it is how we cope with these activities that may well make the difference between success and failure in research. So this chapter is devoted to introducing some basic ideas about them which form the foundation for the whole book. They will be developed in detail in succeeding chapters, but first, let us have a slightly richer version of the diagram, as shown in Figure 1.2 on page 11. This version at least takes the 'before', 'during' and 'after' activities into account.

Before I start discussing the three key stages in this diagram, let me draw your attention to the fact that the process as shown here is not a straight linear one; there is indeed a sequence, but it is not a series of watertight, self-contained stages that are completed one after another. The activities identified here are part of a continuity, and they are returned to and repeated at various points. For example, what we find in the early stages of searching for information is very likely to lead us back into defining and

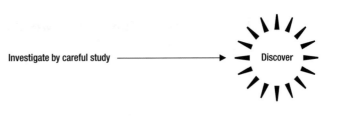

Investigate by careful study ⟶ Discover

Figure 1.1   The dictionary definition of research.

redefining the focus of our research; and we may well make experiments in writing at different points during the research – and this in turn may lead us to identify topics on which we need more information.

What are we looking for?

This stage is often not given due time and thought – yet it is critical for the success of research projects. A recent study (Fister, 1992) of the research processes of undergraduates who had completed successful research projects indicates that for them 'getting a focus for research was the most challenging and the most time-consuming part of the entire project … even for those who had fairly structured assignments'. It is interesting that people who did successful research experienced this; one wonders if in this study those who were less successful with their projects realized the significance of meeting this initial challenge. Certainly my own experience of working with students doing research for the first time suggests that they often have extreme difficulty in formulating what their research is to focus on; and when the difficulty is left unresolved in the hope that it will sort itself out, the outcome is usually not a happy one.

If we start searching without at least a rough definition of what we are looking for, at worst we shan't find anything of use, and at best we may spend a lot of unnecessary time and effort before we find something useful. And if we don't know what we are looking for, we face the problem raised by the duck in its argument with the mouse in *Alice in Wonderland*:

> 'Found *what?*' said the Duck. 'Found *it,*' the Mouse replied rather crossly: 'of course you know what *"it"* means.'
> 'I know what *"it"* means well enough when *I* find a thing,' said the Duck: 'it's generally a frog or a worm.'

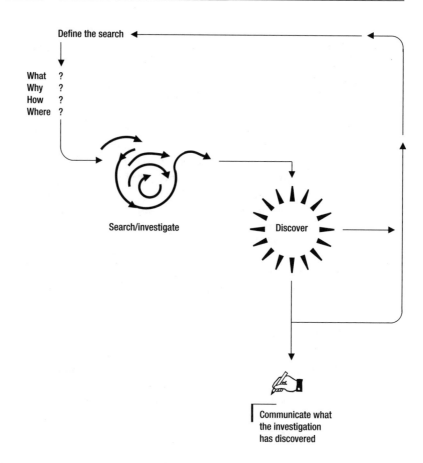

| **Figure 1.2** | The real research process. |

The definition of the 'research focus' need not be a complete and detailed one; the theme can indeed come into focus as a result of preliminary, fairly general searching. But as a starting point we need *some answers* to the questions:

- What am I looking for?
- Why am I looking for it?
- How shall I set about it?
- Where shall I start looking?

Chapter 2 looks in more detail at this stage, from the point of view of 'mapping out' the research territory and identifying the kinds of information that we need before we enter it, and that we shall have to look for in exploring it. Chapter 5 suggests ways of dealing with the situation that can happen at later stages in the research, when everything suddenly and inexplicably goes out of focus in spite of exemplary preparation – often as a result of fatigue and/or isolation.)

Managing what we find

If we don't *manage* the information which we collect during searching, we run the risk of failing to make discoveries, making only partial discovery, missing essential relations between pieces of information, misinterpreting the meaning of what we find. This is because of the characteristics of human memory, which is essentially unreliable. It can make astonishing leaps and connections, but it isn't very good at remembering where it put things, and that can cause great difficulty when we load it with a lot of new information, as we do when we are engaged in research. Hence we need to provide it with some external help in managing the information we are giving it, so that we can easily find from our store of information the articles and notes that are relevant to a particular topic, the quotation that we want to use in the introduction to a chapter, the figures from a report that support a key argument which we wish to make.

Managing the store of research information goes beyond just finding what we want; it is also concerned with helping us to:

- Review our present store of information and spot areas where it's thin and needs adding to
- Identify contradictions (real or apparent) between what we have gathered from different sources
- Verify things that we remember in part but not in detail
- Check if there is support for a 'hunch' or half-formulated hypothesis
- See how our own thinking has developed over a period, what changes it has gone through, what new elements have come into it.

All these are essential and natural activities in research, and to carry them through effectively and without too much trouble we need the support of what Stibic (1982: 1) calls 'tools of the mind' – a range of methods, techniques and applications of technology of various levels that support intellectual work:

> For our purposes, intellectual work can be characterized as working with information – accepting, evaluating, organizing, storage, retrieval, handling, processing, original creation and output information... the work is partly or prevailingly abstract and it contains to some degree an element of creativity.

We invest an enormous amount of research time in finding information; in order to profit from the investment, we need to develop ways of organizing and managing the information store as we build it up. Unfortunately knowledge of the relevant basic principles, which are actually very straightforward, is not widespread, nor is appreciation of simple ways of using information technology in applying them. Chapters 3 and 4 attempt to rectify this.

Communicating what we have discovered

If we did not communicate what we have found, our research would be incomplete. It would not be available as a source of information for others; the knowledge we have gained through it would not be put into the world; and our work would not be available for evaluation by those whose job it is to assess its value and reward us accordingly. A regrettably high proportion of academic research actually meets that fate, and I cannot think of anything more likely to leave a 'creeping bitterness' and sense of failure. A lot of projects that *do* get finished falter badly in the communication stage, yielding products that don't do justice to the underlying work. There are many reasons: regarding the 'writing up' as a separate process, detached from the research proper; underestimating the time and stress entailed in any major piece of writing; lack of experience of creating relevant written products (most people come to writing their dissertation with only the experience of essay writing to sustain them, and I cannot think of any less adequate preparation, indeed, I am not sure what essay writing prepares one for except more essay writing). Chapters 6–10 are devoted to ways of managing the end of the research process which is concerned with transforming the knowledge the researcher has gained from the research into an 'information product' that communicates the knowledge to others who need to use it for their own purposes.

Transformations and the cycle of communication

I have just spoken of 'transforming' knowledge into an 'information product'. *Transforming* is a key concept which underlies everything I have to say in this book, so let me give a basic explanation of what I mean when I apply the term in relation to *information* and *knowledge*.

The long history of the development of the human mind and our power to think and communicate with one another is really a history of transformations.

THE FIRST TRANSFORMATION

The development of the human mind started when the first humans transformed their experience of the outside world into representations of it inside their minds. What set them apart from the apes was their way of doing this.

Apes live entirely in the present, and can remember only individual concrete events, but the first humans extended this power by starting to represent events and feelings through deliberate action – something that survives today as the art form of mime. The representation was both for themselves and to communicate with others. It was the first step in the development of societies with their cultures and customs.

THE SECOND TRANSFORMATION

Next came the transformation from representation by action to representation by spoken language – something that is universal to all humans. The process took hundreds of thousands of years, but by 50,000 years ago language in the form of speech had developed among the humans who were our direct ancestors – probably in Africa.

The interactions between thought, spoken language and society led to more and more invention of language to meet the needs of new ideas and new relationships, and so the transformation of thought and early human society became faster and faster.

THE THIRD TRANSFORMATION

Speech lasts only as long as sound waves reverberate. The next great transformation was of ideas into a form where they could be stored outside the mind in permanent form.

The first step in that process was what Merlin Donald (1991) calls 'visugraphic invention'– the symbolic use of graphic devices. This began about 40,000 years so (Australian aboriginal rock carvings and paintings, for example), but the first truly advanced graphic skills date from 25,000 years ago, as shown in European cave paintings like those of Lascaux and Altamira. While speech is universal to all humans, not all societies developed graphic invention. Again, this new kind of transformation rose to serve the needs of what was most important to humans – finding food (by hunting in this instance) and fertility – and again, it brought new developments in thinking.

The next step in the transformation of ideas into external permanent visible form was writing. Again, this was a development that happened only in some places – initially in Mesopotamia, in response to the needs of a trading society.

The great transformations

Once humans had invented writing, the most important transformations – information outside the mind into knowledge inside the mind and knowledge inside the mind into information outside the mind – became much easier. While you can certainly make these transformations by means of speech, they depend on the people you are communicating with being present. Writing allows communication *across space and time;* because it transforms knowledge into something that can be *stored outside* the human memory, it allows *reflection* and the creation of a *network of learning.*

Writing, as McArthur (1986) explains in his fascinating study of 'lexicography, learning and language from the clay tablet to the computer' made possible new kinds of stores or containers for human knowledge, and networks to connect them. The rate of change constantly speeded up. While it took hundreds of thousands of years for human beings to get to writing, it took only about 6,500 years from writing to printing, and only 500 from printing to computers. And the whole development of computers from scratch to date has taken only 50 years.

Digitized electronic storage and networking of knowledge are the latest in the series of transformations in the 'external symbolic memory' with which humans have learned to support their internal biological memory. They bring incredible expansion of the potential for our minds to think and transform ideas – which we still haven't learned to use effectively.

To summarize, the development of human thinking – *cognitive development* – has always been driven forward by the need for these two reciprocating and interacting transformations:

1 Experience from the *outside world* into *representation* in the mind as knowledge.
2 *Knowledge* in the mind back into *representation* in the outside world as *information.*

Information and knowledge

In speaking of transformation in the intellectual work and communications of human beings, I have used the terms 'knowledge'
and 'information' to stand for *what* we transform. It will be as
well to give an explicit definition of the two here, though I hope
that what I mean by them has emerged from what I have said
about transformation. So ...

| DEFINITIONS   Knowledge and information

Knowledge *is the experience we gain from our encounters with the
outside world of society, nature, and the written and spoken word. We
transform what we find in the outside world, and store it in our minds
in 'mental containers'; it is internal and invisible, and the way we
organize it is individual to each of us; it is a personal possession that
belongs to us more securely than material goods.*

Information *is the visible or audible form into which we transform
our knowledge when we need to communicate it to someone else. It is
knowledge put into the outside world for use. And the way in which
other human beings use it is to transform it back into inward knowledge which belongs to them. And they too engage in the same cycle of
transforming their knowledge into information. Figure 1.3 represents
the basic process in a simple form, but we may imagine that cycle
repeated many times over, to form a network of communications
spreading across space and time. And we become a part of that network when we engage in research.* ▶

These definitions, and the idea of the transformation of information to knowledge, owe a good deal to Brookes (1980: 21), who
regarded 'information as that which modifies a knowledge structure in any way', and defined a knowledge structure as 'a live,
information-seeking ... entity always striving to modify itself to
be in dynamic equilibrium with the information it is receiving'.
A more recent development of the same idea comes from
Ingwersen (1992: 126): 'by transforming the recipient's state of
knowledge, information turns into knowledge – as matter may
convert into energy'.

Brookes (1980: 23) also has an expressive metaphor for the
process of transforming knowledge to information; he speaks of
'the n-dimensional knowledge structure has to be squeezed into a
linear verbal stream (linear in time)', which at the receiving end
is filtered through the user's knowledge structure, and, if communication is successful, 'modifies that structure as the bits find
their proper places.'

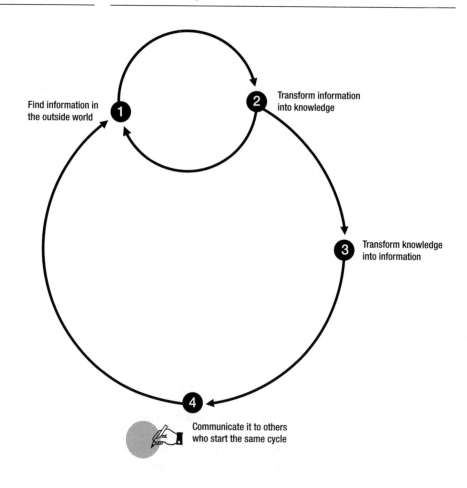

Find information in
the outside world **1**

Transform information **2**
into knowledge

Transform knowledge **3**
into information

Communicate it to others **4**
who start the same cycle

Figure 1.3   The cycle of transforming information to knowledge and knowledge
to information.

So the essence of the searching and investigating that goes on
in research is *transformation*. And two distinct modes of thinking,
acting and being are involved in transformation: the analytical/
theoretical, which is to the fore in collecting information from the
outside, categorizing, interpreting and storing it; and the intuitive/
reflective, which depends on being receptive and open to external
and internal influences, and which can often be promoted by concentration on practical tasks that leave the mind free and quiet
rather than actively striving. Both are necessary; we cannot be in
both modes at the same time, but there is a time for each and

we can come to recognize it, and then their outcomes feed each other to the benefit of what we are trying to do.

A student who had experienced great difficulty and many trials in getting started on her MA in graphic design expressed it like this:

> The left/right opposition or mutual interference between different functions became apparent early on. Attention to ordering received ideas in language (inspiring, confusing, verbose, banal), listening to lectures, reading and then writing – blocked any visually creative flow. The muse of visual exploration did not want to play. And I was finally compelled to shut up the mind's several voices and pay heed to my intuition which spoke to me in the quiet pre-language voice of its authority. To follow where it led, side-stepping the voices of anxiety, intellectual scepticism and analytic enquiry.
>
> Once evaded, impossible to recall at will: as intuition walked me, in darkness, in silence, sensing my way.   (CHASSEAUD, 1993)

Once she had recognized the two modes, she was able to allow each its due time, and the final result was a truly mature piece of work that benefited from both. Readers of Keats's letters may be reminded, as I was on reading this passage, of his definition of *Negative Capability*, ... 'that is, when a man is capable of being in uncertainties, mysteries, doubts, without any irritable reaching after fact and reason ...' (letter to George and Thomas Keats, 1817, in Forman, 1942: 72).

Unwarranted attempts to force research, particularly in the humanities and social sciences, into an old-fashioned 'scientific' mould still continue, despite the fact that physical science long ago moved away from the idea of '"Truths" based on a methodology of deductive reasoning in the face of a systematically collected body of evidence ... it is noticeable that the social sciences, sociology, psychology, economics, have tended to cling neurotically to the old nineteenth-century view of science'. (Graves, 1994)

Research as a 'contract'

I hope that by now we have gone some way to answering the question 'What are we doing when we "do research"?'.

We are asking ourselves questions and using the answers to define what we are looking for; we are gathering information in the outside world that will enable us to discover what we seek; we are managing the information we gather so that it yields us the maximum help; we are transforming information into knowledge, and knowledge back into information for others; we are drawing on both active/conscious and reflective/intuitive modes of thought; we are participating in a great network of human communication.

One final answer takes us back to a practical level: when we undertake a research project of any kind, we are entering into a 'contract' – an agreement first of all with *ourselves*, and then with the institution where we do the research, as represented by our tutors or supervisors. The agreement is usually an informal one, though I have worked in one or two institutions where there is an actual formal contract drawn up by students in consultation with staff (an extract from one such contract is given in Chapter 4, pages 70–72). In essence, the researcher undertakes to carry through a defined piece of work, with specified objectives, using appropriate methods, and to deliver an agreed product (a dissertation, thesis or project report, for example) which will meet institutional standards, to a fixed time limit. The institution (and this bit is not usually very specifically stated) for its part, implicitly at least, undertakes to provide supervision, access to necessary facilities, and competent evaluation of the products submitted.

The importance of regarding research as a contractual undertaking (especially as one that we make with *ourselves*) is that it encourages researchers to question themselves at every stage, to define, clarify and document what they are doing, and to schedule their activities realistically. More than that, a formal contract can allow them to propose the terms on which their work is to be evaluated – the contract quoted in Chapter 4 does this, and in order to gain the advantage of this, students have to do a great deal of useful thinking, at the start of the course and at various stages during it, about their objectives and methods, and about the outcome of their work.

References

Brookes, B. C. (1980) Informatics as the fundamental social science. In P. Taylor (ed.) *New trends in documentation and information.* Proceedings of the 39th FID Congress. London: Aslib.

Chasseaud, A. (1993) 'Transformations and the Hate Object', unpublished MA dissertation. London: Central St Martins College of Art and Design.

Donald, M. (1991) *Origins of the Modern Mind.* Cambridge, Massachusetts: Harvard University Press.

Fister, B. (1992) The research processes of undergraduate students, *The Journal of Academic Librarianship,* 18 (3): 163–169.

Forman, M. B. (ed) (1942) *The Letters of John Keats.* Oxford: Oxford University Press.

Graves, J. (1994) 'The hitch-hiker's guide to the unconscious mind', unpublished paper.

Ingwersen, P. (1992) Information and information science in context, *Libri,* 42 (3): 99–135.

McArthur, T. (1986) *Worlds of Reference.* Cambridge: Cambridge University Press.

Stibic, V. (1982) *Tools of the Mind.* Amsterdam: North Holland Publishing Company.

2 | Mapping the research territory: known and unknown areas

The last chapter outlined the key activities of research:
- Asking ourselves questions and using the answers to define what we are looking for
- Gathering information in the outside world that will enable us to discover what we seek
- Managing the information we gather so that it yields us the maximum help
- Transforming information into knowledge, and knowledge back into information
- Drawing on both active/conscious and reflective/intuitive modes of thought
- Participating in a great network of human communication
- Entering into a 'contract' with ourselves, and with the institution where we do the research.

Questions to ask at the outset

Now it is time to look in detail at the questions researchers need to ask and answer at the outset in order to give themselves a first 'map' of the territory they are about to enter, and some guidance on paths they can follow through it. So this chapter is concerned with these questions:
- What does the research seek to find out? What questions does it aim to answer, or what hypothesis does it seek to test?
- What areas of knowledge, subjects and disciplines will the research need to draw on?
- What do we know already that is relevant? Where shall we need to add new knowledge and/or know-how?
- What are the likely sources for the required information?
- What are the potentially useful ways of doing the research – the 'methodological options'?
- What limits must we set to the breadth and depth of the inquiry?
- What obligations do we have to fulfil to the institution in which we are doing the research?

What this chapter is not about

I should emphasize before going any further what this chapter is *not* about – it doesn't deal with the initial selection of a research topic or area. (That stage is well covered elsewhere – see, for example, Bell, 1993: 15–23.) It assumes that you have identified a broad topic, defined a theme, and made some investigations to see if it is a feasible one for you, and whether anyone else has covered the same ground before. Here, I shall be talking about mapping the area once you have decided on it.

End products

The end product may literally be a 'map' or diagram – a graphic presentation of the territory; or it may be a document – a research proposal, or a 'statement of intent' or a 'contract' – which forms an agreed point of reference for both the researcher and the people to whom he/she is responsible. It is important to be aware of the alternative ways of doing the job; there is no single best one, and the thing to aim for is a method with which you feel comfortable, and which fits in with any requirements of your institution.

I shall deal with the subject by means of three examples, from real research projects. I hope that they will show the kinds of question the researchers asked themselves and the use they made of their answers in mapping their research territory. I have selected them because each takes a different approach, and each researcher finishes up with a different kind of 'map'.

> **Example 1**
> A major research project undertaken in the final year of a first degree in Development Studies

What does the research seek to find out?

The research addresses an area of public concern: the use of pesticides and the need for a reduction in levels of use. The focus for the research is the process known as 'integrated pest management' (IPM). Two concepts are involved in it: integration of pesticide use with other methods of control (for example, biological, use of resistant plant strains), and economic thresholds (ETs)– that is, the point at which it becomes economic to start applying measures of pest control. Until comparatively recently, the method has been implemented in parts of the world where the crops are of high value and where there is a reasonably well-established basis of agricultural research and advisory services. Now, however, IPM is being promoted in many developing countries, for low-value subsistence crops.

Problems have been encountered in applying the idea of integrated pest management in these situations. It has been suggested in the literature that difficulties in getting information about economic thresholds may be one of a complex of elements giving rise to these difficulties. It looks as though it would be worth investigating the nature and possible causes of the problems more thoroughly.

So the research area has been initially defined as 'The causes of observed difficulties in applying integrated pest management '. Given that this project has to be done in the context of a first degree in the UK, without the possibility of visiting developing countries, would it be feasible to look at what local East Anglian farmers are doing with economic thresholds? They have access to good services, appropriate insecticides, etc. Are they aware of thresholds? If they are, are they following them? If not, why not?

It looks as though this would be a promising line to follow, because, during the second year of the course, with this in mind as a possible major research project for the third year, the student carried out a small pilot survey of East Anglian farmers (nearly two-thirds of whom maintained that they would use insecticides at the first sighting of any pest, without waiting for the density to reach a prescribed threshold – even though many of them were aware of such thresholds!).

The relevance to developing countries is that if farmers with many advantages still don't use economic thresholds, there's little chance of resource-poor farmers using them. So the investigation might lead to alternative strategies, which could be tried out in developing countries.

Research questions and hypothesis

If that approach is taken, the research questions will be on these lines:

1 Are East Anglian farmers aware of recommended ETs for various common insect pests?
2 How do they make decisions about timing pesticide applications?
3 If they are aware of but don't follow ETs, what factors act to prevent them?

And the hypothesis to test will be:
While many East Anglian farmers have a reasonable idea of specific thresholds for common pests, they will be unable/unwilling to apply them because of various perceived practical limitations.

What are the relevant areas of knowledge?

The areas of knowledge on which the research will need to draw include:
- Agricultural development studies from relevant countries; especially studies of attempts to promote IPM.
- Literature about IPM and ETs.
- Literature about pesticide spraying practices in UK, especially East Anglia; information which is made available to farmers from agricultural advisory services.
- The student's own findings from a small pilot survey of East Anglian farmers in her second year.

What do we know already that is relevant? Where shall we need to add new knowledge?

Relevant knowledge comes from the background reading already done, and from the findings from the pilot survey done in the second year. In this case, because interviews and a questionnaire look as though they are likely options (see below) questionnaire design needs to be added, along with training in use of packages for simple statistical analysis. Interviewing skills already exist thanks to the student's work background in the police force.

What are the likely sources for the required information?

Library, tutors (especially those who have done relevant consultancy assignments in developing countries). Agricultural advisory service. NFU (National Farmers Union).

What are the potentially useful ways of doing the research?

Given that this project seeks to test a hypothesis by studying a random sample of people, and that it is looking for fairly straight-forward factual information, together with some rather 'softer' opinions, it looks as though a questionnaire would be a suitable instrument. Since the sample will be a fairly small one (40 farmers), it should be possible to administer the questionnaire in the course of a structured interview, with the researcher filling in the answers, rather than sending it out by post with the risk of getting a low return. The questions will be mainly ones with yes/no answers, but some will need to be open-ended, to allow respondents to express their own views in their own terms. There is also the point that the course requires students to gain experience of quantitative methods, and of using appropriate software to analyse findings, and this would offer a suitable occasion.

Before the questionnaire is designed and interviews are undertaken, the main reading should be completed, so that the interviewing is done on a basis of maximum awareness. Existing contacts with the local NFU and the farming advisory service will also need to be extended and developed, both to give a sound basis of current knowledge, and to establish communication links for feeding back results of the research when it is completed.

What limits must be set to the breadth and depth of the research?

The time available and the proportion of marks awarded for the project are the factors that will determine how far the research should be taken. The dissertation counts for 40 credits in an academic year during which students are required to complete a total of 120 credits. The deadline for completion is the middle of the second term of the final year of the degree course. (For advice on managing the time available, see Chapter 5.)

What obligations to the institution have to be met?

The undergraduate dissertation is a compulsory piece of work (upper length limit 9,000 words), which must be submitted on time, by the middle of the second term of the final year.

○ END OF EXAMPLE 1

| **Example 2**
An MA graphics research project

This was undertaken as a joint piece of research by two students on a four-term MA course. They had elected to take up a project offered by a large firm in the computer industry which regularly sponsored projects for this course. In this instance, the sponsor was seeking guidance on the use of icons in interactive computer systems. While the students had a strong background of education and experience in graphic design, particularly as applied to designing informative products, the whole field of human-computer interaction (HCI) was a new one for them, and they undertook this project with the aim of getting to know it, and if possible establishing a foothold in the territory for graphic designers to establish themselves.

This particular course requires students to develop what it calls, rather grandly, a 'Statement of Intent', over the first two terms of the course. The statement represents the students' intentions in undertaking their research, and it forms the basis for another document, prepared towards the end of the course – the Assessment Contract (the contract presented as a follow-up to the Statement of Intent quoted here is reproduced in Chapter 4). This example shows how 'Wolfgang 2' (the style the students adopted to refer to themselves – they were actually both called Wolfgang!) made use of the documents they had to prepare, in order to answer the basic questions, map their research territory, plot their course through it, and finally focus the attention of their assessors on the most significant aspects of what they had done.

Statement of Intent

Project title: Human-computer interaction. A study of icons from a graphic design perspective.

Aims of project: To find out how the discipline of information-oriented graphic design relates to the discipline of human-computer interaction, and how it can contribute to improve communication between human and computer in general and in icon-based communication in particular.

Relationship between the aims of the project and the aims of the course:
As this project is being done for an outside client, it will contribute to the objective of being able to implement, plan, schedule, evaluate and respond to client requirements and decisions.

It will contribute to the objective of understanding the use of different media and the implications of technological change, and, as it involves entry into an area where graphic designers have so far had few opportunities to contribute their specialist knowledge, it will involve us in communicating ideas to other professional groups.

As the research is being done jointly, it will contribute to the objective of being able to work supportively with others and to awareness of the dynamics of interpersonal relationships.

Project programme, including methods to be used and timetable of work:
- **Term 1**
- Briefings from client and hands-on experience of the software products in which client proposes using icons.
- Develop plan for sharing the work, and methods for joint working.
- Literature review of research findings on HCI and use of icons.

- **Term 2**
- Examination of icons as currently used in relevant interactive software products from other companies.
- Start on classification of icons.
- Gain hands-on experience of using desktop publishing software.
- Begin writing dissertation – chapters on the HCI background.

- **Term 3**
- Use desktop publishing software to design icons.
- Analyse problems likely to arise when DTP software is used for this purpose by non-designers.
- Develop solutions and test with fellow-students.
- Finalize classification of icons.
- Continue with dissertation.

- **Term 4**
- Design and produce classification of icons.
- Write, design and produce guidelines for icon design.
- Complete dissertation.

Details of work to be submitted
- A visual classification of icons for use as a reference aid by software application designers and graphic designers.
- Guidelines for the design of icons for software application designers and graphic designers.
- Dissertation.

Resources and materials that will be needed for the research
Briefing and contact person in client firm which has offered the project.

Tutorial support needed
Graphic design tutor with experience of icon design in context of information design; tutorial advice on presentation of written work in dissertation.

○ END OF EXAMPLE 2

> ## Example 3
> A PhD research project in information science

The research project on which I am currently working grew out of my experience in a variety of jobs. In earlier years I worked as an editor of informative texts (technical books and journals), then on two occasions I had the job of setting up and managing a publishing programme for organizations. This brought me into contact with the processes and technologies by which information products were actually produced, and into working with a designer whose specialism was planning the visual presentation of such products, and specifying how the production should be managed. It also gave me a useful insight into how organizations managed (or mismanaged) this side of their activities.

In the course of the second of the two jobs mentioned, I went to college part-time and studied information science, because the job also required me to set up and manage an information service. In 1979 I decided to work independently as an information consultant, taking as my particular specialism the territory that spanned my two areas of interest: getting and organizing information that people need for their work, and presenting it to them in visible forms that they can use easily. I have gone on working in that territory ever since, in co-operation with my designer colleague, and we have written articles and a book to give expression to our thinking on the subject. My consultancy work with organizations has given me many further incidental insights into how they manage, or fail to manage, the ways in which they present information about themselves and their work to the outside world and to their own staff.

What does the research seek to find out?

Given this background, when I decided it was time to do some research, I chose as my topic 'The role of information products and information presentation in organizations' and as the main research question:

Is it possible to trace and identify links between, on the one hand, how the processes of creating information products and presenting information are managed, and, on the other, consequences to the organization, in terms of achievement of strategic objectives in such matters as information flow, communication, cost-effectiveness and efficiency?

What are the relevant areas of knowledge?

Figure 2.1 shows the rough map I made of the research territory, on the basis of experience. I indicated on it the connections as I saw them between the key sets of topics, and the points at which it seemed there *ought* to be connections in a properly managed organization, but at which there might well not be. Then I used the map to help me with the other essential preliminary activities.

What do we know already that is relevant?

I have, as explained above, a good deal of actual experience of how organizations deal with these matters, gained partly as an employee and partly as a consultant. This is also an area where I have tried to keep up to date for the past 15 years, so I have collected and indexed quite a lot of material in my own database. That made my starting point. I used the experience to draw up a set of research topics relating to the various areas on the map:

- What organizations do at present in the way of presenting information:
- For internal use
- For communication with their 'outside world'
- Whether they have a specific strategy that relates it to their key objectives
- How they relate their information products to the management of their information resources
- Who takes the decisions on information products
- Management attitudes towards information products and presentation
- The people who do the work of creating the products: how they are trained, and how they do the job
- The technologies used
- The relationship between those responsible for in-house design and production of information products, and those who control relevant IT systems
- How information products are costed
- How they are evaluated
- Whether organizations lose by not exercising unified control over the quality and appropriateness of their information products, and the nature of the loss.

I also did a search on my database, using such terms as *information policy, information products, information design, desktop publishing, electronic publishing, information presentation,* which

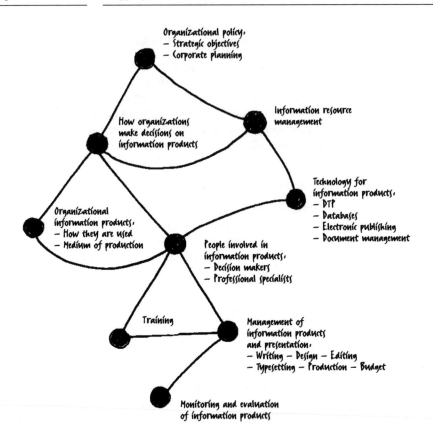

Figure 2.1   A first map of research territory. Project title: *The role of information products and information presentation in organizations.*

yielded a set of about 50 references (for more about setting up a database of useful articles, etc., see Chapter 3, pages 43 to 58). I put them to one side for rereading, and following up useful references, but it was quite obvious from a casual glance that the area where I had least information was on the side of the technology and actual hands-on designing. The reason for that was simple: I had always used my designer colleague as my information source there – I knew he kept up to date with the technology, used it intensively, and thought constantly about its design implications. So here was an area where I would have to deepen my own knowledge and do a lot more reading for myself, guided if possible by advice from well-disposed designers. It might also turn out to be necessary to take some training myself, as a non-designer, in the use of desktop publishing – to get a feel for the experience of many of the people I would meet in the course of doing case studies.

What are the likely sources for the required information?

Other people were clearly going to be very important in pointing me to useful sources for extending and deepening my own knowledge, and in fact one of the steps I took, once the research proposal had been accepted, was to start letting them know about it through the newsletters of specialist groups. I wrote a short article for the newsletter of the Information Design Association, and a note for a network of people especially concerned with the management of information resources.

At the same time, I did the more conventional things associated with starting a literature search – in this case a visit to the Science Reference and Information Service of the British Library, a subject search on the British Library's database of British reports, translations and theses, and a search on the appropriate abstracting services. I was fortunate in having a basis in my own collection to start me off; it gave me useful terms for the searches and provided a background against which I could evaluate how useful the items that came up were likely to be.

What are the potentially useful ways of doing the research?

Given the theme of the research, the ways of doing it were fairly obvious. It depended on having access to real organizations, talking to the people with various kinds of responsibility for information products, and being able to observe for myself what went on. So the key bit of methodology would have to be the case study – another reason for talking to lots of colleagues, because they might provide leads to useful organizations, or even invite me into their own! Given that I was interested in the particular, and not trying to do a survey or gather quantitative data, I rejected the idea of using a questionnaire pretty quickly (encouraged by the advice of experienced colleagues), and decided to do case studies as I had done them in the past for books, by means of carefully planned interviews and reading material supplied by the organization.

It also seemed sensible to make an early start on the case studies, and to spread them over a period of time (a practical move, because I would have to be ready to fit in with other demands on the time of the organizations I was approaching). Since I already had a fairly good foundation of reading in the field, I decided against a preliminary period devoted solely to library work; I would probably get more from 'interleaving' the reading with the case studies.

One other bit of methodology suggested itself: I had for some time been interested in action research (where the researcher is both observer and participant), and it seemed that perhaps the final phase of the study might usefully be devoted to some action research in one or two organizations, to try out some of the tentative conclusions from the case studies. I was encouraged in that by a colleague whose PhD thesis I had helped to edit; he had a lot of experience in action research, and could be used as a live resource as well as a guide to the literature. This too was an area in which I would need to add new knowledge and know-how.

What limits must be set to the breadth and depth of the research?

As the emphasis is on informative products, I decided to avoid advertising and public relations products so far as possible. The research is being done part-time, and, while I have set myself a target to complete it within five years, the main aim in this case is to do the job as thoroughly as may be, and to look at everything relevant. One other restriction does exist, however: in making case studies in companies and institutions, I am dependent on their goodwill, and so I am under an obligation to get the information I need with as little demand as possible on their time. That requires careful preparation on my part, so that interviews do not overrun the bounds of patience

What obligations to the institution have to be met?

The first obligation to be met in this case is, during the first year of the research, to 'produce an identifiable, independent piece of work which will be used by the Board of Studies to assess progress and suitability to transfer ... from MPhil to PhD'.

Given that I had decided to make an early start with case studies, and had set up a handful in the early months of the first year, it seemed a first set of case study reports would be a good way of meeting this requirement. It fitted in with the programme I had set myself, and would form a distinct piece of work which could be used to assess my progress and the quality of the work. For purposes of assessment, it had the advantage of demonstrating not only how I organized ideas and put them in writing, but also how I managed interactions with the case study organizations.

     ●   END OF EXAMPLE 3

From mapping to starting to manage information

The examples of mapping research territory in this chapter show the transition that researchers make from defining the questions they seek to answer, to identifying the knowledge they require, and to deciding on likely sources of relevant information which they can transform into knowledge and apply to answering the research questions.

     The next stages lead out into the world where the required information is dispersed, and bring researchers face to face with looking for what they need; 'making it their own' by reading and note-taking; acquiring and creating physical items of information (photocopies of articles, books, their own notes); and managing the constantly growing collection. So the next chapter is devoted to those processes.

Reference

Bell, J. (1993) *Doing Your Research Project. A guide for first-time researchers in education and social science* (2nd edn). Buckingham: Open University Press.

3 | Managing information to support research

'I wish you would let me sort your papers for you, uncle,' said Dorothea. 'I would letter them all, and then make a list of subjects under each letter'.

(GEORGE ELIOT, *Middlemarch*, 1871, Chapter 2)

Dorothea's uncle was suffering from a problem that affects many researchers – he had 'documents' which he had collected when a question struck him (as they did at frequent intervals), but, as he confessed, 'they want arranging.' I have often tried to visualize what his niece was proposing to do (she didn't get a chance of trying it out), and I have come to the conclusion that she was working her way towards a subject index. The way she planned to start was a sensible one, except that, if she lettered the documents, when she got to the 26th she would have run out of letters – now, if she had *numbered* them ... but I am getting ahead of the subject of this chapter.

My experience as an information specialist in teaching students about coping with the information they collect and create while doing research shows that they quickly become aware of such questions as:

- How do I get something useful out of a source that I know has something relevant somewhere?
- How do I use my time cost-effectively in taking notes and selecting quotations?

As the files of notes grow and the photocopies of articles accumulate, they run into new problems:

- How do I store all this so that I know where I've put things?
- When I want to write up a section on a particular subject, how do I find everything that's relevant to it in the material I have collected?

In other words, they want to know how to get a good return on the time they have invested in finding useful information, in terms of being able to get into the store of information by any way in they need, move about in it easily, find everything relevant, and miss nothing that's potentially useful.

This is not going to be a chapter about how to use library catalogues or on-line databases; most institutions of higher education now provide instruction in these essential skills, and, should this be lacking, individual librarians – if approached with courtesy – are usually willing to point students in the right direction and help them find their feet. What I shall be advocating and trying to pass on is ways of *thinking about information,* and practical techniques of applying the thinking, that are characteristic of the disciplines known variously as 'information science', 'librarianship', 'information management', or 'information studies'. (If this happens to be your own subject area, feel free to move on if you wish, though I hope you will stay with me and give what I have to say the benefit of critical attention – and indeed let me know if you have alternative ideas or comments.)

The domain of information science

The practitioners of those disciplines – often described today as 'information professionals' – are particularly concerned with such activities as:

- Defining the *information* that is needed to achieve given purposes
- *Finding* it through using knowledge of a wide range of likely sources
- Transforming it from the way it is when we find it in the 'outside world' into *knowledge* inside the mind of the individual
- Storing information outside the mind in *external memory*
- Helping people to get to the stored information they need
- *Adding value* to information by presenting it in forms that match the needs of those who want to use it.
- *Applying information technology* to help in all these processes.

That list of activities demands an enriched repetition of the definitions of knowledge and information which were given in brief form in Chapter 1 (page 16), as they are essential for understanding much of the rest of this book:

DEFINITIONS

Knowledge and Information

Knowledge *is what we acquire from our interaction with the world; it is the results of experience organized and stored inside each individual's own mind in a way that is unique to each (though there are features common to how we all do it). It comes in two main kinds: knowledge about things, and* know-how. *We make it our own by* transforming *the experience that comes from outside into internal knowledge. Knowledge belongs to us more surely than most of our possessions, and is indeed the most precious and essential of all possessions.*

Knowledge also depends on memory – *and memory too comes in two kinds:* internal – *inside our heads, and* external – *knowledge put into external stores like libraries or databases or reference books so that we don't have to try to carry everything we need in our heads.*

Information *is what we* transform *knowledge into when we want to communicate it to other people. It is knowledge made visible or audible, in written or printed words, or in speech. We can also usefully think of it as the* food of knowledge *because we need information and communication to nourish and maintain our knowledge and keep it in good shape for what we need to do in the world. Without the food of information, knowledge becomes enfeebled.* ◗

The transformation of information into knowledge, and knowledge into information, forms the basis for all human learning and communication; it allows ideas to spread across space and time, and links past and present in a network that embraces generations and cultures over milleniums – Figure 3.1 gives a simplified representation of the process.

The parallel between the domain of information science and what researchers have to do

Chapter 1 defined what researchers do as: asking questions with the aim of defining the scope of their investigation and the information they will need; managing the information they find; and transforming the information they gather into internal knowledge. So there are close parallels between what information professionals do, and what researchers need to do. Researchers, too, need to:

- Define their information needs
- Locate sources of potentially useful information to meet the needs
- Transform the useful information they find into internal knowledge
- Store the physical objects – like books, photocopies of articles, photographs, results of experiments – that embody useful information
- Manage their store of useful information, so that they can get into it easily, move around it quickly, and find what they need whenever they need it.

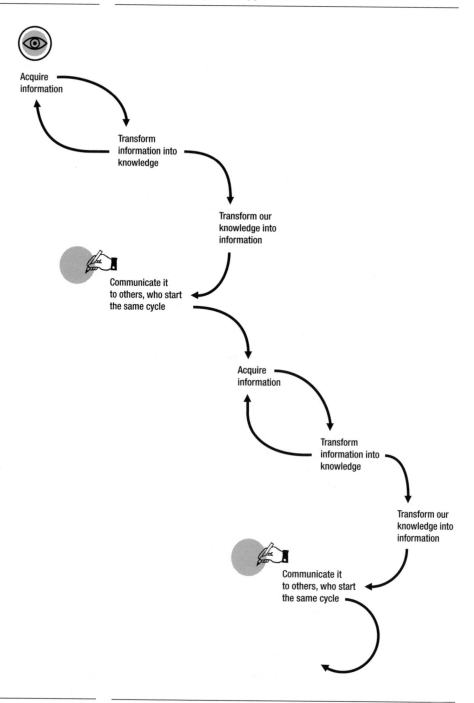

Figure 3.1   Transforming information into knowledge and knowledge into
information – the chain of human communication.

[37]

Towards information management

The rest of this chapter is devoted to some ideas (drawn from the theory and practice of information science) about practical ways of dealing with those research activities that are specially devoted to information. I should emphasize before we go further that there is no one 'right way' of doing it, and successful researchers use a wide variety of strategies. All I claim for what I am suggesting is that it is based on what I have found to work for me in my own research, and that it seems to act as a useful starting point for students in various disciplines and at different stages of their studies, from which they can go on to develop strategies that suit their own ways of working. I hope that you will work through the processes I suggest in the next few pages for yourself, using material from the subject area of your own research project. All you will need in the way of equipment is cards, paper, and something to write with.

Preparing to go fishing for information

Once you have a 'map' of the area of your research (see Chapter 2, page 30), there is something very simple you can do, which will give you a tool that can be used in various ways throughout the rest of the process of research.

If you would like to try it now, take five minutes to jot down on a piece of paper a handful of words and phrases which sum up for you the key topics of your research; they may be subjects, the names of authors, or organizations, or places, or historical periods. Now put each separate word or phrase at the top of a card (A6, 148 x 105 mm is a good size).

The example in Figure 3.2 is based on an actual project on systems done recently by second-year BA Product Design students. Their brief was to get acquainted with the considerations involved in presenting information on screen to the public, to design the essentials of a system for giving local information to tourists in London, and to produce drawings for specimen screens. Figure 3.2 shows a typical set of terms produced by the process described above.

The very action of identifying important topics in your own words, and writing them down, brings those words to the front of your mind, where they can act as a set of 'hooks' that you can trawl over the surface as you scan books, articles, etc.; while the connections between the ideas they embody start to make a kind of net that helps you to pick up related ideas as you read, and to

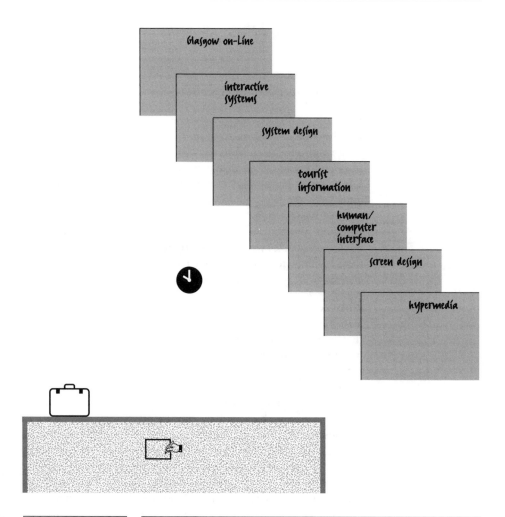

Figure 3.2   Key topics on cards.

spot other links, so that the network gets richer as you go on. The dissertation from which I quoted in Chapter 1 (page 18) throws an interesting sidelight on this metaphor, and the part which 'unconscious knowledge' plays in the process:

Paul Klee's approach to everything he did was in conscious recognition of knowledge the unconscious already possessed. His forays, his journeying enquiries could be described as 'fishing expeditions'... Perhaps the original question mark, held in conscious focus, is in itself enough to trawl, unseen, the deeps of an unconscious questing, unhindered by the restraints of a linear march of reason.

(CHASSEAUD,1993)

[39]

Figure 3.3 shows the terms of Figure 3.2 in the guise of hooks suspended from a net.

Locating sources of information

YOUR OWN COLLECTION

I find it useful when starting on a project to begin with what I have readily to hand – my own collection of articles, press cuttings and books. It's a manageable size, and less daunting than setting off straight away for a library. Looking at a familiar set of items with the key topics in mind usually reveals things I'd forgotten I possessed, or that I had not thought of as relevant to this particular project; and rereading them gives me clues to other books and articles worth looking up in a library. So I have something definite to look up when I go to the library, rather than starting from cold and feeling clueless.

FINDING USEFUL LIBRARIES AND INFORMATION COLLECTIONS

Your research topic may well require some kinds of information that are not fully covered in your college library. Useful first steps in your own library:

1 See what the library has in the areas you have identified in your your 'research map', paying especial attention to the periodicals, because they are where the most recent information about relevant research, new ideas, and developments in particular fields appears (a useful starting point is *Willings Press Guide*, which gives details of journals and other regularly appearing publications), and to relevant reference works and directories.

2 Look at reference works that will point you to libraries and collections specializing in your topics, these two in particular:

• *Aslib Directory of Information Sources in the United Kingdom*. This two-volume work is the most comprehensive general reference source for the United Kingdom (and it also has a section on European Union information sources).

• *Guide to Libraries and Information Units in Government Departments and Other Organizations*. A valuable source for specialist collections, this one is indexed by organization and by subject.

3 Look at directories that list associations which specialize in particular areas, to locate any that work in the fields of interest to you; the most useful are:

• *Directory of British Associations*. This lists national associations, institutes, etc., including those concerned with particular industries, technologies, etc.

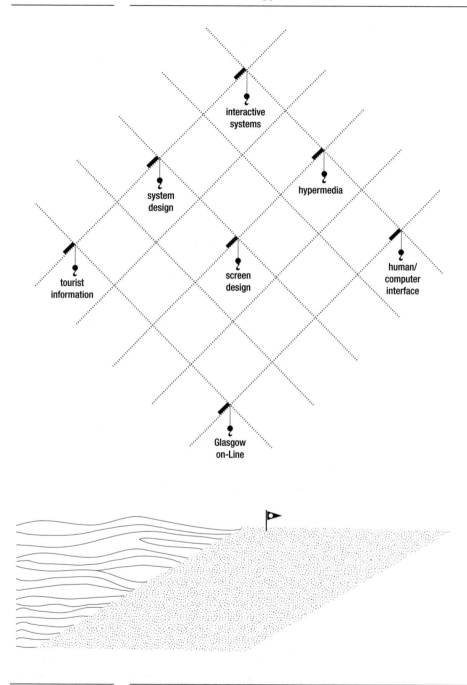

Figure 3.3   Going fishing for information.

- *Councils, Committees and Boards.* From the same stable, this is a directory of advisory, consultative, and other bodies in UK public life.
4 Look at directories of electronic sources of information; two useful general ones are:
- *The CD-ROM Directory.* Published by TFPL.
- *Gale Directory of Online Databases.* Published by Gale Research.

PEOPLE AS SOURCES OF INFORMATION

Research is not just a matter of reading in libraries; some of the most worthwhile information comes from listening to people who have specialist knowledge. First among them are the information professionals in the libraries and other collections you use. While it is obvious self-preservation if you are doing research at any level to know how to get into the catalogue and to find your way about the reference shelves and the periodicals stacks, librarians as a professional group are usually glad to share their specialist knowledge of their collections with enquirers who know what they are about, and can formulate their questions clearly. You will certainly need their help if you plan to make on-line searches on databases.

Then there are the people who work in the fields in which you are interested, and have knowledge and know-how relevant to what you are trying to find out. Tutors or fellow-students will often suggest people to approach, and when you have found one such person, he or she will often point you to others who can be helpful. Reading in your subject area is another source; some of the most valuable personal contacts I have made in the course of writing books, for example, have been with authors whose work I have found matches and extends my own ideas.

However you come across them, approach people who are potentially useful to you with care and courtesy. They have other things to think about besides what concerns you, and the more potentially helpful they are the busier they are likely to be. So give them a clear, brief explanation of your research project, why it seems that they could be helpful, and what you are asking of them. An introductory letter is probably the best way, as it gives time for reflection. Telephoning is a useful first approach, however, if you want to find who is the appropriate person to write to in an organization. And never omit to thank people who respond to your requests – even if the response turns out to be not particularly useful for your purposes.

When sources yield useful items of information

The moment when we find a source that contains material which is relevant to our interests is sometimes when our troubles really start. The sheer physical volume, and the way in which it is all too often presented to the reader, can be overwhelming. (We can learn useful things for our own writing from analysing what makes other people's difficult to understand – see Chapter 8.)

Extracting information from printed and on-screen sources is a very exhausting process. However, there are ways of making it manageable and productive. This is where the 'hooks' for fishing for information begin to come into their own. They are useful first of all in looking at indexes – to books, and to abstracting and indexing services in your subject areas – and at library subject and author catalogues.

When you start scanning actual text that may contain relevant information, if you have a small number of key words or phrases in mind as you read, you will find that they leap off the pages as you scan. When they do, that is the point at which to start reading with attention. It is also the point at which you start thinking about whether you need a photocopy of the item, or whether it is sufficient to take your own notes.

Putting someone else's key facts and ideas into your own words is a good way of helping to transform them into knowledge in your mind. A whole chapter could be written about note-taking, but I am going to say just four practical things here:

1 If you decide that notes are enough, the first thing to do is to make an *accurate* note of the *bibliographic details* of the item: for periodical articles – author, title of article, name of journal, volume and part number, date, and pages on which the article appears; for books – author, title, publisher, place and date of publication, and ISBN (International Standard Book Number, a unique identifier).

2 At the top of your notes about any item, put, in colour or large letters, the key topic from your list on which it has useful information (usually you will find that any one item has useful information on more than one topic; see Figure 3.4 on page 44 for ways of dealing with that).

3 Resist the temptation to copy large chunks of text mechanically; it is less tiring and more useful to copy for possible quotation only those sentences and phrases which say something important in a way that cannot be bettered – and when you do that, note the page number from which the quotation comes,

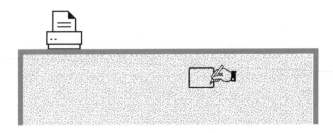

> Geographical Information Systems (GIS)
> Land Use
> Natural Resources Management
>
> Deane, G ((1994) The role of GIS in the management of
> natural resources, Aslib Proceedings 46 (6) , 157–161
>
> GIS – 'a system for capturing, storing, checking, integrating,
> manipulating, analysing, and displaying data which are
> spatially referenced to the Earth' (157)
> Applications include , emergency planning, management of
> urban areas, land use planning, resources management.
> Case studies of applications in developing countries & EEC.
> 'Data acquisition, input and maintenance are likely to be
> more significant in the longer term than the cost of
> purchasing the GIS' (160)

Figure 3.4

Using cards for notes. Doing it like this allows you to bring together material on key topics, and ensures that you have complete and correct bibliographical details of every item on which you take notes. It also allows you to remind yourself of other topics on which items have useful information.

so that anyone who reads the quotation in your ultimate report or thesis can easily find it in its source.

4 There are various 'vehicles' for notes: notebooks, loose leaf binders, cards. Whichever you use, the first thing is to get the bibliographic details right (see above). If you use notebooks, *number the pages* (see Figure 3.5), and number the notebooks too, as their number grows, which it will. With loose leaf binders and cards, put each set of notes about a particular item on a separate sheet or card; if they need more than one, clip or

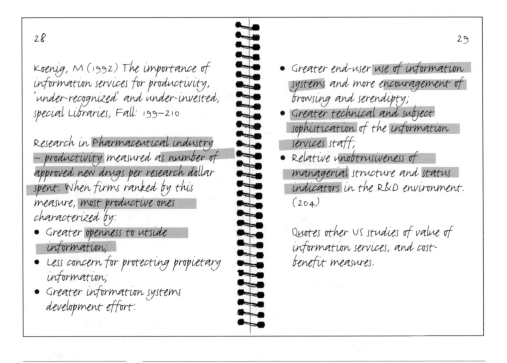

28

Koenig, M (1992) The importance of
information services for productivity,
'under-recognized' and under-invested,
special Libraries, Fall: 199–210

Research in Pharmaceutical industry
– productivity measured as number of
approved new drugs per research dollar
spent. When firms ranked by this
measure, most productive ones
characterized by:
• Greater openness to outside
  information;
• Less concern for protecting propietary
  information;
• Greater information systems
  development effort:

29

• Greater end-user use of information
  systems and more encouragement of
  browsing and serendipty;
• Greater technical and subject
  sophistication of the information
  services staff;
• Relative unobtrusiveness of
  managerial structure and status
  indicators in the R&D environment.
  (204)

Quotes other US studies of value of
information services, and cost-
benefit measures.

Figure 3.5   If you use notebooks, number the pages, highlight key topics, and enter
complete bibliographic details of the items on which you take notes.

staple them together. There is a lot to be said in favour of using
separate sets of sheets or cards for each set of notes, rather
than running them on in a notebook – if you keep them as separate sets, you can treat your own notes in just the same way as
you treat photocopies of articles, etc. There is more about this
later, when we come to look at making 'keys' to the information store (page 49).

If you take photocopies of articles or pages from books, put the
key topics on the first page (see Figure 3.6 on page 46).

Whether you make your own notes or take photocopies, use a
highlighter to mark key sentences (Figure 3.5). That helps you to
absorb the important information, and when you return to the
material later on, the highlighting will focus your attention on the
relevant passages and save you time in rereading.

All the things I have been describing are a help in transforming
external information into structured knowledge which belongs to
us. We can't, however, rely on remembering everything we have

Figure 3.6   If you keep photocopies of articles, note the key topics on which they have useful information, and make sure all the bibliographic details are on the photocopy!

found, so we need to help ourselves to get back to the actual information whenever it can be helpful in what we want to do.

For that, we need methods for *storing* the actual items of information we gather – books, articles, pictures, our own notes, etc. – and we need *keys* for getting into the store so that we can manage the information to our own benefit. In what follows I shall first go through the process of doing all this 'by hand' – because this is the best way of making the steps and the thinking that lies behind them clear. Once again, I hope you will think it worthwhile taking time to try out what I am suggesting for yourself, using actual items relevant to your own research. After that, it will be easier to explain how computers can make the process less time-consuming and more effective.

Storing your information

It takes a little self-discipline to have a place for everything, and to put everything in its place – but it is worth the effort. Collecting information demands a large investment of time and trouble, so it is a pity to give yourself extra trouble by leaving it in a disorganized heap, where it is accessible only with a lot more trouble, and even when you have taken the trouble you can't be sure you have found everything relevant. So choose suitable containers for the things you collect or create, for example: folding boxes for reports, sets of notes, photocopies of articles, etc; shoeboxes for cards with notes; plastic covers in ring-binders for photographs, etc.

❙ DEFINITION

Two definitions relevant to storing information: *items* and *records*

1 *An* item *– for our purposes here, it means a physical object that carries information, for example: a book, an article, a picture, a set of notes, a map.*
2 *A* record *– something that stands for an item, and that can be used to represent it when we are thinking about the information that the item contains. A record may be a material object such as a catalogue card in a library, or it may be held electronically in digitized form in a computer.* ❱

Then you have to decide how to *arrange* the items in their containers. There are two choices: either grouping like with like, or just adding them as they come in – the most recent next to the last one you put in. (In fact you may find it convenient to store some things in one way and some in the other. In my current research project I am doing case studies in a number of organizations; I keep a box for each organization, and put the publications I am given for it into the box. At the same time, I treat other items I collect, like relevant articles, in the second way.)

If you choose the first, then you will need to label each container and the items you put in it with the name of whatever main grouping you decide is appropriate (the list of key words/phrases (see page 38) that you made should help in this). If you choose the second, then you will have to give each item a number in sequence (and if you do that, it is good sense to keep a checklist in numerical order in a notebook, so that you can easily check what number to allocate next, and can also identify any missing item).

Whichever you choose, there are problems – problems which have, indeed, formed one of the main concerns of librarians for the last century or so. In the next section, I shall explain what they are, and try to suggest some ways of minimizing them, under the heading of 'Keys to the store'.

DO YOU NEED RECORDS OF THE ITEMS YOU COLLECT?

For the moment, there is one other question to consider in relation to storing items of information: Do you need to create records (see definition) for your items – for example, when you collect an article or a book, should you make out a card for it, with bibliographic details and perhaps a note of the main subjects it covers, like a library catalogue card? My own view is that, if you are managing a collection that can be called a library – even a small one – by manual means you do need records in order to meet the needs of users for information. But if you are just concerned with your own collection for your own use, then you can save yourself the trouble of making out cards, *provided you do two things:*

1 Make sure that every item is clearly labelled with all its *bibliographic details,* and with the *key topics* on which it has information that is useful to you (see page 46).

2 Give yourself an *index* to your collection of items. I shall explain why this is necessary, and how to set about it, in the next section. For the moment, here is a definition.

| DEFINITION

An index *is a tool (usually in the form of an alphabetically arranged list of terms) that points to all the different places in a single item (like a book), or in a collection of items, where you will find information about a given subject, person, place, etc.* ▶

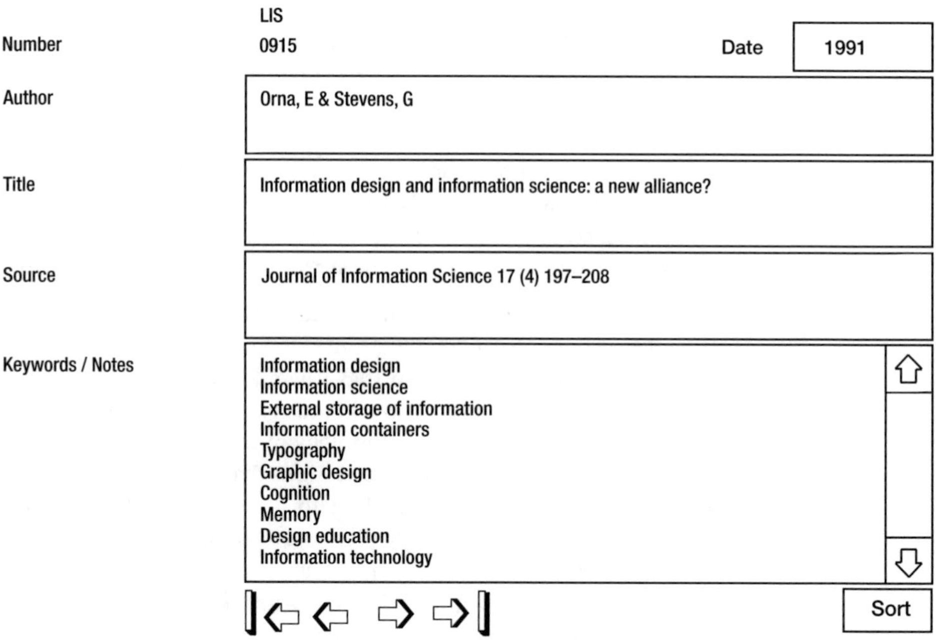

Number	LIS 0915		Date	1991

Author	Orna, E & Stevens, G

Title	Information design and information science: a new alliance?

Source	Journal of Information Science 17 (4) 197–208

Keywords / Notes	Information design Information science External storage of information Information containers Typography Graphic design Cognition Memory Design education Information technology	⇧

⬅| ⇦ ⇨ ⇨ |⬅   Sort

Figure 3.7

If this were stored only under Information Design, I wouldn't find it if I were looking for information on Cognition or Memory, yet it has useful material on both these topics.

Keys to the store

The awkward feature about any kind of arrangement, and the one which causes the problems I mentioned above, is that, by the very fact of bringing items together in *one* way (by author, by main subject, by date of addition to the store, for example), it separates items that have *other* things in common. The same author may have written articles on a number of quite different subjects, so while that arrangement makes it easy to find everything by a given author, it makes it hard to find items on a given subject. An article which is principally on one main topic may also contain material on a number of other topics, so arranging items according to their main subject means you are likely to miss them when you are looking for information about the other subjects they deal with (see Figure 3.7 for an example). Arrangement by date of addition allows you to see quickly the most recent or the earliest items, but not much else – the items you collected this week are likely to be by a range of different authors, and on a variety of topics.

Antonio Crestadoro (1856) made a wise observation about the consequences as they affected readers in the British Museum Library over a century ago:

> Freedom is, in all things, an essential condition of growth and power. The purposes of readers in search of a book are as manifold as the names and subjects, or headings under which the book may be traced. Entering the book only once is giving but one of its many references and suppressing the remainder.

His solution was to enter a shorthand version of the book's details under *all* the relevant headings, in a kind of grand master index to everything in the library, so that it would be found whenever it would be useful in answer to all kinds of purposes. It was a good solution, though with the technology of the mid-nineteenth century it would have taken a lot longer than the 'short time' he claimed it would take to apply it to the contents of the British Museum Library. (It is very pleasant to think that Crestadoro's ideas are today finding a modern interpretation in the On-line Public Access Catalogue of the new British Library.)

However, it is a solution that can work very well for the materials that individual researchers collect, using nothing more than the means that were available 150 years ago. This is how you do it:

1 Take the set of cards on which you put your key research topics (see Figure 3.2 on page 39).
2 Take the items you have collected.
3 If you are arranging your store by adding items as they come in and numbering them in sequence:
    put their numbers on the relevant cards (see Figure 3.8).
    If you are arranging items in subject groups:
    put their main bibliographic details and the name of the subject group in which you have filed them on the relevant card (see Figure 3.9 on page 52).

Now if you want to find all the information you have on one of your key topics, you can see from the cards which are the relevant items, and you can find them by going direct to the containers (see Figure 3.10 on pages 53–54). When you get to the items, your highlighting (see page 45) will allow quick scanning and finding of the important content.

As you see, numbering items is time-saving both in putting away and in indexing, and it makes sure you will find everything relevant to a topic.

A grouped arrangement takes longer to index thoroughly. On the other hand, if you don't bother to index, you can take a short-

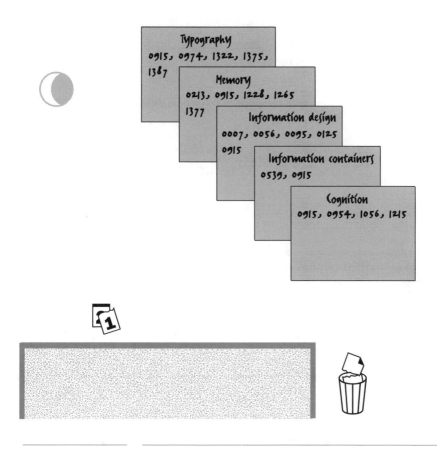

Figure 3.8   Some of the topics of Figure 3.7 used as headings on cards, with the numbers of the items which deal with these topics.

cut and find the main relevant items by going direct to the container with the name of the topic you want – but you will miss other relevant items which are stored under different main topics. In this, as in most of life, there are no free rides.

If, like many people, you use notebooks a great deal, you may like to deal with them by making a rough 'back-of-book' index to them. Write your list of topics in alphabetical order, leaving plenty of space between them, in the back pages of each notebook. Then put alongside each topic the numbers of the pages which deal with it (see Figure 3.11 on page 55). The extra work of making a separate index is one of the prices one has to pay for the convenience of using notebooks rather than making separate sets of notes which can be treated like printed items.

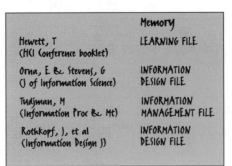

| Figure 3.9 | One of the topics from Figure 3.7, with details of relevant items. This time the items are not stored in numerical order, but grouped in boxes according to a main topic, so you have to put some brief bibliographic details and their location on the index card. |

Managing the information store with the help of information technology

Everything that I have described so far can be done with nothing more advanced than pen and ink, paper and cards, and I hope you have followed the suggestion of trying it for yourself, because that is the best way of seeing how it works. The essential element is effective human *thought* about the subjects in hand, the questions we want to ask, and what we want to do with the results. Once we have sorted out our ideas, however, we can speed up and simplify the process of managing information, and enrich the quality of thought by sensible use of information technology. For an entertaining, common-sense, yet scholarly survey of what to aim for in a personal computer-based information system, read the articles by Cawkell (1991a; 1991b), who offers advice based on years of experience about how to arrive at a system which reduces indexing time to a minimum, yet 'provides a just acceptable retrieval performance' – which will still be a great deal better

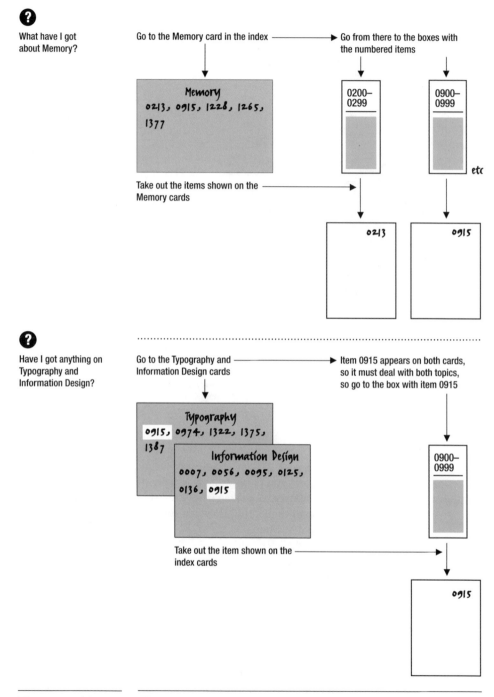

❓
What have I got
about Memory?

❓
Have I got anything on
Typography and
Information Design?

Figure 3.10 (a)　　Finding information from an index to items which are arranged in number order.

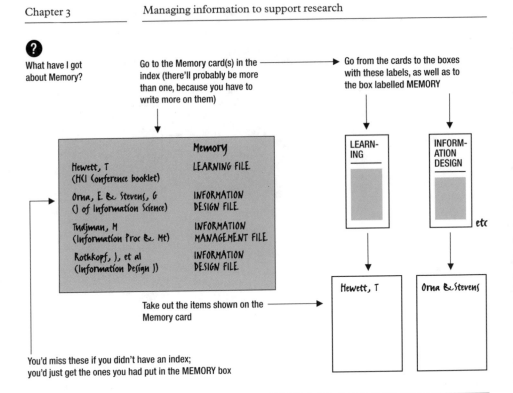

What have I got about Memory?

Go to the Memory card(s) in the index (there'll probably be more than one, because you have to write more on them)

Go from the cards to the boxes with these labels, as well as to the box labelled MEMORY

Memory

Hewett, T
(HCI Conference booklet)   LEARNING FILE

Orna, E & Stevens, G
() of Information Science)   INFORMATION
                                    DESIGN FILE

Tudjman, M
(Information Proc & Mt)   INFORMATION
                                   MANAGEMENT FILE

Rothkopf, J, et al
(Information Design))   INFORMATION
                                  DESIGN FILE

LEARN-ING

INFORM-ATION DESIGN

etc

Take out the items shown on the Memory card

Hewett, T

Orna & Stevens

You'd miss these if you didn't have an index;
you'd just get the ones you had put in the MEMORY box

Figure 3.10(b)   Finding information from an index to items which are arranged by main topic.

than what you would get from 'an unsorted pile of ... journals, books, catalogues, reports, etc.' (Cawkell, 1991a).

There is a lot of reliable software for managing information on personal computers nowadays, usually described by the generic name of 'database packages' or 'text-retrieval software'. These are the main things that they can do to help with the activities I have been describing:

- They make it simple to enter details of items of information, including the key words, your own notes, and quotations from them.
- They can find and show you items that deal with particular topics, are written by specific authors, etc.
- They allow you to make 'combined' searches for items that have a specific combination of features – for example, *reviews* of productions of *a particular play*, with a given *actor,* in the years *1870–73,* in *Edinburgh and Glasgow.*
- They can print out lists of items on particular topics, etc.

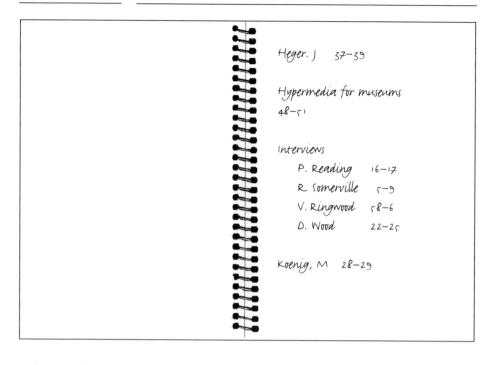

Figure 3.11   Extracts from a back-of-book index to a notebook.

For these advantages, all you have to do is plan a record form (yes, you do need one if you want to manage information on a computer) that takes into account the kind of items you need to gather in your research, and the kind of questions you want to answer from the collection. Figure 3.12 on page 56 shows examples from two typical databases. In these examples the software is Hypercard on a Macintosh computer, but the principles are very much the same for other software on other machines. It is also possible to link this database or text retrieval software with software that can handle photographs, graphics and audio material.

If your college provides facilities for using a computer to handle information arising from research projects, these are the steps you need to take:

1 Make a list of the kinds of item you want to store on computer, for example:

- Records of articles, books, etc.
- Names and addresses of useful organizations, suppliers, individuals, etc.

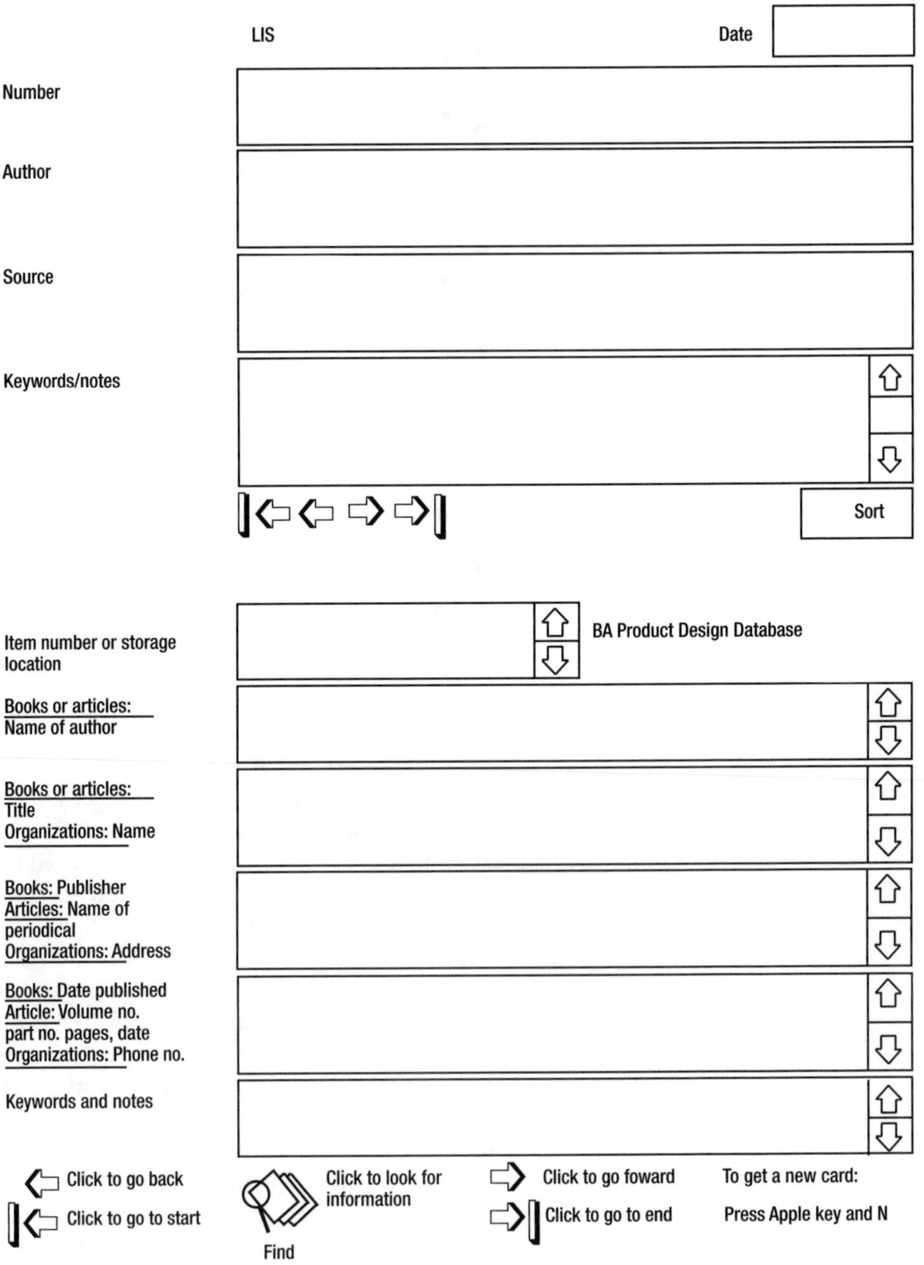

LIS   Date

Number

Author

Source

Keywords/notes ⇧ ⇩

|⇦ ⇦ ⇨ ⇨| Sort

⇧ ⇩   BA Product Design Database

Item number or storage location

Books or articles:
Name of author ⇧ ⇩

Books or articles:
Title
Organizations: Name ⇧ ⇩

Books: Publisher
Articles: Name of
periodical
Organizations: Address ⇧ ⇩

Books: Date published
Article: Volume no.
part no. pages, date
Organizations: Phone no. ⇧ ⇩

Keywords and notes ⇧ ⇩

⇦ Click to go back
|⇦ Click to go to start

Click to look for
information

Find

⇨ Click to go foward
⇨| Click to go to end

To get a new card:

Press Apple key and N

Figure 3.12 (a) & (b)   a) Record from a database for handling bibliographic items (using Hypercard).

b) Record from another Hypercard database; this one was designed to be used by a group of students, to allow them to input details of books, articles, and organizations.

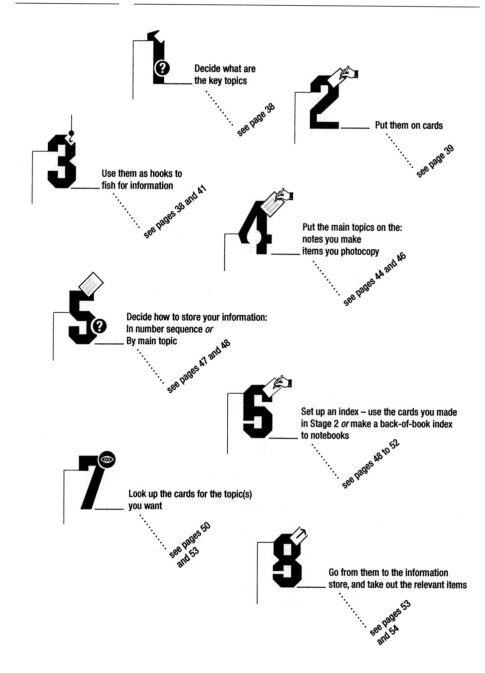

1 Decide what are the key topics
see page 38

2 Put them on cards
see page 39

3 Use them as hooks to fish for information
see pages 38 and 41

4 Put the main topics on the:
notes you make
items you photocopy
see pages 44 and 46

5 Decide how to store your information:
In number sequence *or*
By main topic
see pages 47 and 48

6 Set up an index – use the cards you made in Stage 2 *or* make a back-of-book index to notebooks
see pages 48 to 52

7 Look up the cards for the topic(s) you want
see pages 50 and 53

8 Go from them to the information store, and take out the relevant items
see pages 53 and 54

Figure 3.13   The process of indexing and searching: a visual summary of doing the whole job manually. If you use a computer for holding records and finding information, stages 1–5 still apply; for stages 6–8 see pages 52 and 54–58.

- Graphic and/or audio material.

2 Identify typical questions you will need to answer from your store of information.

3 On paper, design a rough record form that covers the features which you will need to include in your records in order to be able to answer the typical questions.

4 Then consult the advisers in your computer centre about appropriate software for your purposes. If you can be guaranteed access to the computers when you need them (if you can't, it's not worth the trouble), learn how to use the available software to set up your database, input records, search for information, and print out the results.

5 When you have set up your database, maintain it regularly, and *never* forget to keep an up-to-date backup copy.

The whole process of indexing and using the index to locate items with required information is shown in pictorial form in Figure 3.13.

References

Cawkell, A. E. (1991a) Ideal personal information systems, *The Intelligent Enterprise,* 1 (8): 14–18.

Cawkell, A. E. (1991b) Managing personal information systems, *Critique,* 3 (8): 1–12.

Chasseaud, A (1993) 'Transformations and the Hate Object', unpublished MA dissertation. London: Central St Martins College of Art and Design.

[Crestadoro, A.] (1856) *The art of making catalogues of libraries or, a method to obtain in a short time a most perfect, complete, and satisfactory printed catalogue of the British Museum Library* by A reader therein. London: The Literary, Scientific & Artistic Reference Office.

4 | Keeping the record straight: documenting the research

Introduction

It is all too easy, once a research proposal has been accepted, to dive into the serious business of gathering information and to forget about relating what we are doing to either the 'research map' or the time-scale we established. Researchers who do that are not getting value out of the investment of good thinking time they put into the early stages of planning. They don't get the benefit of seeing how what they find relates to their first thoughts; and they miss the opportunity of redrawing and updating their map and making it into a better guide for the next stages. They also run serious risks – of missing the path and falling into the Slough of Despond; of failing to see and remedy in time flaws in their original reasoning; and of getting their time scale irreparably out of balance.

So this chapter is about setting points at which we deliberately pause to:
- Compare what we are doing with what we planned to do
- Check how we are keeping to the initial timetable
- Bring the 'research map' up to date
- Identify new questions and new directions to investigate.

It is also about the records we need to keep which will allow us to do these things.

If we do that, we can make good use of positive developments, happy accidents, and new thoughts, as well as taking timely corrective action. More than that, if we record the results as we go, we give ourselves a 'chronological trace' (in some courses it is called a 'research diary') of the evolution of our thinking, and that can help us not only to evaluate what we are doing, but also to develop first tentative conclusions, and to get a perspective of the whole process when we approach the end of it.

A record of how thinking has evolved can also be a source of strength and reassurance at those awful times which most of us experience at some point in doing research, when we feel everything has gone out of focus, the original clarity of our intentions has disappeared and we no longer know where we are going.

Such times are in reality potentially creative ones; the mental discomfort is likely to be the manifestation of rather more new experience than can comfortably be coped with at once, or of the conflict between analytical/theoretical and intuitive/reflective modes described in Chapter 1 (page 17). It is easy to lose nerve when what had originally seemed clear and certain starts dissolving into confusion. But if we can accept the inner turmoil and turn outwards to look at what we have recorded about the development of our thinking, we can find there clues to the changes and strands to follow that will gradually, given time, come together to form a new synthesis.

Things to record and keep

Here is a basic checklist of items that researchers should keep where it is easy to find and refer to them:

THE DOCUMENT THAT DEFINES THE RESEARCH
The research proposal, statement of intent or whatever else it may be called by particular institutions. This constitutes the original 'contract' for the research and as such is a precious document. It may well go through more than one version in the preliminary stages – a provisional and then a final statement, for instance – and it may be amended at some later point. However many versions are produced, keep a copy of each, labelled with the date on which it was written and the date on which it was approved.

This is the source document, and it has multiple uses; it contains your original definition of the research area and of the questions the research will seek to answer, the methods you propose to use, and the outcomes you seek to achieve from the research. From that source you can derive a multitude of other useful products as the research proceeds; the key ones are described below, and shown graphically in Figure 4.1.

Don't look on your research proposal as a tedious chore that had to be undertaken to feed the academic bureaucracy with the pieces of paper it demands in large quantities. It is something you should be thoroughly familiar with, which you keep going back to, and which you use constructively.

It can also be an important defence against ignorant interventions by those who are less aware than they should be of the nature of what you have undertaken to do. A few years ago, there was a change in course leader of an MA course on which I was a visiting teacher. The course was in an institution recently formed

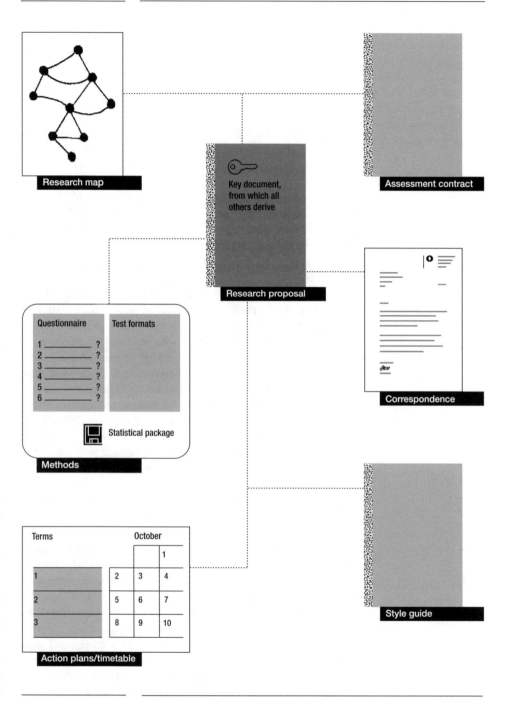

Figure 4.1   Documents derived from the research proposal.

by a merger between two colleges in the same field of study, but with very different traditions. When the original course leader left to go to another job, it was in the second term of a four-term MA which had been established some years before in one of the two component colleges, then an independent institution. He had been instrumental in developing a course with a clear structure and philosophy, which attracted students who found it congenial to their research interests. His replacement came from the other college, and brought to the job – besides a good deal of sheer incompetence – a determination to make his mark in this promotion by speedily overturning as much as possible of what he considered to be an out-of-date and fuddy-duddy philosophy, and replacing it with something more appropriate to modern trends in the discipline concerned. Not being much given to studying the rules of the institution, he did not appreciate that students already doing the course had entered into it under the terms set out in the existing 'course document', and were therefore entitled to complete it on those terms, and in accordance with the research proposals they had agreed at the start of their course.

Within a few days of his arrival, he made it his business to interview each of the students – interviews in which he did most of the talking while they got little chance of explaining what their projects were and how they were progressing. The sequel was expressions of dismay on his part at the nature and quality of the projects, and then almost total neglect of this group of students, while he busied himself with planning off the top of his head a new course structure and philosophy (expressed, perhaps fortunately, in such impenetrable language that nobody could make any sense of it).

Fortunately the existing students were mature and well motivated, so they kept on working conscientiously, but they were obviously anxious about what harm the course tutor might do to their prospects. As the time for the assessment of the MA work drew near, their anxiety increased. They had not had the normal opportunity for a preliminary individual and group meeting with the external assessor of the course, and they feared that the course tutor might seek to influence the assessor against them. In this unhappy situation, there were fortunately some positive points: the students worked well together as a group and supported one another; the external assessor was an independent-minded person who had acted in that capacity for the course over the past two years; and an assessment contract had been introduced at the beginning of that year.

The students had drawn up their own contracts which set out clearly the nature of their projects, their objectives in doing the research, and the criteria by which they considered it was appropriate to assess what they presented. The contracts were given to the external assessor in advance, and the students were able to base their preparations for presenting their work and answering questions about it on what they had stated in the contracts. In the event, although the course tutor was one of the internal members of the assessment panel, he was unable to muddy the waters, because the assessment contract constituted a reference point to which both students and assessors could address themselves.

In this instance, the existence of a clear piece of documentation prepared by the students about their own research actually enabled them to defend themselves against what could have been a damaging attack on their work, leading to unmerited failure.

RESEARCH MAP

Any graphic or written interpretation you derive from the research proposal which sets out the paths you plan to follow, the areas to explore, the links you will seek to make (see Chapter 2). This, too, will change as the work advances: unknown territory will become familiar, blank areas will begin to be filled in, more paths and connections will be added, and possibly some ground will be abandoned. When there are major changes, revise the map; don't discard the earlier versions, but keep a complete series in date order, so that you can see how the project has evolved over time, what you have done, and what remains to do. Figure 4.2 on page 64 shows a revision of the research map of Figure 2.1.

DECISIONS ON METHODS

Keep a record of how and why you decide on methods for your research, of how they develop, things you learn from actually trying them out; if methods don't work, record the reasons why, and the modifications made in response to finding that they don't work.

Keep master copies of the materials you develop for applying your chosen methods, for example: questionnaires, interview schedules, background information for people who are to be interviewed, experiment design, protocols for carrying out experiments, formats for recording the results.

If you decide to use formal statistical methods for analysing any of your findings, record what they are, and the sources they

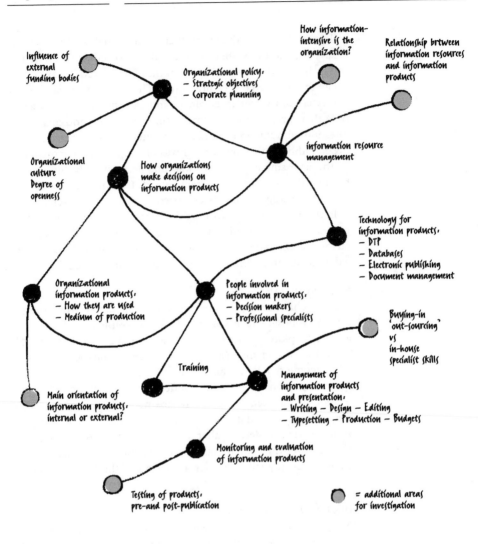

How information-
intensive is the
organization?

Relationship brtween
information resources
and information
products

Influence of
external
funding bodies

Organizational policy.
— Strategic objectives
— Corporate planning

information resource
management

Organizational
culture
Degree of
openness

How organizations
make decisions on
information products

Technology for
information products.
— DTP
— Databases
— Electronic publishing
— Document management

Organizational
information products.
— How they are used
— Medium of production

People involved in
information products.
— Decision makers
— Professional specialists

Buying-in
'out-sourcing'
vs
in-house
specialist skills

Training

Management of
information products
and presentation.
— Writing — Design — Editing
— Typesetting — Production — Budgets

Main orientation of
information products.
internal or external?

Monitoring and evaluation
of information products

Testing of products.
pre-and post-publication

= additional areas
for investigation

Figure 4.2   Revised map of research territory (see Figure 2.1). Project title: *The role of information products and information presentation in organizations.*

are derived from; and if you are going to use a computer in making the analysis, record the software considered, the final decision, and your reasons for it.

If you do this, when it comes to writing up your research, you will have in accessible form just about everything you need for the section on methodology that usually has to form part of a research report or thesis. It will be separate from the findings you get by applying the methods, which will be recorded elsewhere and reported in a different part of the final product.

PLANS OF ACTION/TIME SCHEDULES

Chapter 5 is devoted to ways of managing the available time for research so that you get the best out of it. Making action plans, estimating the time that activities will take, and planning how to integrate them so as to make best use of time, is of course an important part of that.

Here, I shall just anticipate the full treatment of the topic by emphasizing that it's essential to keep the major plans and timetables that mark key stages in the research: the original ones that form part of the research proposal or are drawn up on the basis of the proposal; significant modifications to them; and plans and time schedules for key individual sections of the work (such as case studies or series of tests).

> **Example 1**
> Part of a preliminary plan for a research project
> scheduled to be completed within three terms

Term 1: major activity – survey of relevant literature:
- Start from preliminary survey made in last year's project
- Follow up citations in articles included in that
- Establish key themes related to research topics
- Explore other relevant areas, including methodology for case studies and for testing
- Preliminary write-up of literature survey.

Towards end of term:
- Put together criteria for case study organizations
- Compile first list
- Start making contacts and set up pilot interviews.

During vacation:
- Carry out pilot interviews.

Term 2: major activities:
- Complete literature survey. Use literature survey to define themes/questions for case study interviews
- Carry out case studies. Use findings from case studies to extend literature survey
- Establish format for reporting on case studies
- Plan product for testing on basis of findings from case studies and literature survey
- Contact sample of organizations and arrange tests.

During vacation:
- Develop product for testing
- Establish test format
- Outline structure for dissertation, decide on information elements needed, develop standards for presentation.

Term 3:
- Finalize product for testing
- Carry out tests
- Establish format for reporting test results
- Draft report of findings from tests
- Draw conclusions and draft chapter on implications of test results
- Finalize drafts already written
- Write introductory and concluding chapters
- Prepare illustrations
- Edit dissertation.

⬤ END OF EXAMPLE I

Each main bit of planning breaks down into smaller stages, with their own plans and timetables – those are more ephemeral, important while you are doing the work but not necessary to keep once it is completed (see Chapter 5 for the time-management aspect of this).

TUTORIAL REPORTS

You will be supported, guided, impeded, neglected, tormented, or cheered (the whole range is possible) by one or more tutors who have the responsibility of supervising your research. Meetings with them should lead to agreed decisions, recommendations for action, suggestions for changes. They should be the occasion for constructive interchange of ideas, and the results should be recorded. In some institutions, it is the tutor's responsibility to give the researcher a written report of decisions made,

Meeting of 11 03 1993

Subjects discussed:

Organization of the final product.
Agreed that it will consist of a series of short 'books'
about the key themes of the research.

Typical form of each book:
1 Main text.

start trying
this out with
'The book of
the hand'

2 Relevant 'background' text which readers should
   be able to see on facing pages to main text.
3 References and reading list, at the end of each book.
This form will influence decisions about page structure.

Experiment with page layout & type faces

Information elements for which style decisions have to be
made:

see sketches in
Notebook 3 for
some icon ideas

- Footnotes – asides to main text *marginal*
- Icons, acting as symbols for key themes treated
  in more than one 'book'; a device to help readers
  to follow a single theme through many books if they wish
- Headings – a simple hierarchy, probably with only
  two levels
- Quotations and references – in text, and in reference list.

Figure 4.3   An annotated tutorial report.

things to be done before the next meeting, etc. If that is not the
case for you, then make it your responsibility to keep a record of
meetings and of action you agreed to take; either way, record
what you did as a result.

Figure 4.3 shows a tutorial report annotated by the researcher.

CORRESPONDENCE ARISING FROM THE RESEARCH
Most research projects involve the researchers in writing letters –
to institutions they wish to visit, experts they need to consult,
organizations where they wish to carry out interviews, tests or

case studies. Keep copies of all individual letters, and file the replies with them, so that you have a complete chronologically arranged file of your correspondence with any institution or person (and when you go on visits, take the relevant correspondence file with you, so that you can remind yourself and the people you are talking to of your previous discussions). I find it helpful to have the correspondence beside me when I make telephone calls to people in response to letters, so that I can make notes of the points discussed on the relevant letter.

Often it is necessary to produce a standard form of letter that is sent with minor modifications to a number of recipients; keep a copy of it on file for reference – if it's possible to keep it as a word-processed file, you can edit it with the appropriate additions and amendments each time you want to send it to a new destination.

An index of names and addresses of contacts you make in the course of the research is another essential bit of documentation. If you are a Filofax addict, you will add them to that; but I find that a separate index devoted solely to research contacts is easier to use. It can be either a card index with handwritten or typed cards, or the computer equivalent; I keep mine as a Hypercard stack. It's worth the effort of noting on the cards any main events in your dealings with the people they refer to, as shown in Figure 4.4 on page 69.

DECISIONS ABOUT THE STYLE OF THE END PRODUCT OF THE RESEARCH

This again is a preview of something treated more fully later on (see Chapters 7–9). As the research proceeds, ideas and questions about the ways of presenting the final product should start to arise. How much, for example, will it be appropriate to write in narrative form? What kinds of diagram and illustration will help to make points clear? What are the best ways of handling the particular kinds of numerical information that are emerging from the research? And does the institution impose any constraints on presentation that you will have to observe?

It's worth recording your thinking about such questions from the point when you have accumulated a reasonable amount of material from reading and other activities. I find it useful to annotate an outline contents list with first ideas of the ways in which the content of different chapters might be treated. From these beginnings, you will be able to develop a final 'house style' covering all aspects of how the final product will appear on the printed page – a guide that embodies the whole range of

Research case studies contacts

Name	Chalmers, Ian
Address	The UK Cochrane Centre Summertown Pavilion Middle Way Oxford OX2 7LG
Phone/fax	0865 516300 Fax: 0865 516311
Notes	Letter of 10 January 1994. Willing to co-operate: contact = Dr Andrew Herxheimer. Also contact Trever Sheldon at Centre for Health Economics, York YO1 5DD. 23 08 94: conversation with him, agrees to participate 07 07 94: conversation with A Herxheimer; willing to take part. See notes of meeting of 19 08.

Figure 4.4   A card from an index of research contacts, held on a database.

necessary decisions, which you can keep beside you as you write, and which will save you from having to take decisions on the spur of the moment (and probably being inconsistent), and from wasting time checking how you treated a particular element last time. (For more about the design of major information elements, see Chapter 9, pages 153–161.)

DOCUMENTATION THAT GOES IN WITH YOUR SUBMISSION
In many institutions, researchers are required to submit, along with their final report or thesis, some other formal document which acts as background to the work for the people who will make judgements on it. The Assessment Contract mentioned earlier in this chapter (pages 62–63) is an example of a document which performs this function. In this particular institution, it is developed from the Statement of Intent. Submitted shortly before the final assessment of their work, it allows students to give a full description of the work they have done. It also gives them the opportunity of telling the examiners what weight they wish to be given to the various elements of work that they are submitting. The examiners use the Contract as a checklist against which to compare the actual work, and as a guide in assigning marks to the different elements submitted.

Even if you don't have to produce something as formal as this, it is a useful exercise to answer this kind of question as preparation for the oral examination on your research.

| **Example 2**
| An assessment contract

The two students who presented this example used the contract to give the assessors some additional information – about the things they were *not* aiming to do, about what they considered to be unique features of the products of the research, and about the criteria they considered appropriate for assessing it.

Project title

Human-computer interaction: A study of icons from a graphic design perspective

Aims of project

To find out how the discipline of information-oriented graphic design relates to the discipline of human/computer interaction, and how it can contribute to improve the communication between human and computer in general and icon-based communication in particular.

Objectives of the project

1 To transform the complex subject of HCI, which is almost entirely elaborated by specialists, such as systems analysts, system designers, psychologists and human factors specialists and written about in their terminology, into a manageable, structured, informative and understandable piece of information for non-specialists in this subject area. Thus our work is mainly directed to software application designers and information-oriented graphic designers.
2 To provide these users with a clear and understandable piece of background information, necessary for understanding the implications involved in the use of icons for HCI.
3 To provide them with a set of guidelines for the design of icons.

Things we are not seeking to do:

We are not designing the interface of a computer system.
We are not investigating current dialogue styles.
We are not claiming that icons are the ultimate means of communication between users and an interactive screen-based computer system.
We are not making any judgement on good or bad icons.

New ground which we are covering in the project

Links between subject areas: to our current knowledge, no study has been conducted that deals with the implications of HCI from an information-oriented graphic design perspective.

End product

The study is a unique piece of information which can be used by non-specialists in the subject area such as graphic designers to familiarize themselves with the subject of HCI in general and the use of icons as a means of interactive screen-based communication in particular.

Icon reference

To our knowledge, there does not exist a structured and classified compilation of icons on paper. We have put together such a compilation, which can be used by software application designers and information-oriented graphic designers as a reference aid. The essential advantage of an icon reference on paper is that allows a more convenient and faster comparison of different icons.

Criteria which we want our assessors to use in deciding if we have met the brief and achieved the objectives

Criteria in terms of dealing with the client:
- Questioning the brief
- Analysing the client's needs
- Educating the client
 Criteria in terms of the procedure for tackling an unfamiliar subject area:
- Analysis of the problem
- Search for relevant information

- Analysis of information
- Structure of information
- Interrelation of the structured information
- Putting relevant issues in context

Criteria in terms of transformation of findings into a visual form:

- Legibility
- Clarity of information structure
- Comprehensiveness
- Informativeness
- Explicitness

O END OF EXAMPLE 2

Keeping the documentation

We all have our own preferences when it comes to storing our documents. One of my colleagues has shelves and shelves of impeccable box files, each labelled in the same typeface (he's the one who also girds himself up for a stint of work by polishing his desk); another is content with battered old cardboard folders, that have been through several reincarnations. I come somewhere in between. Table 4.1 suggests some forms of storage of proven usefulness for various kinds of documentation.

Documentation	Form of storage
'Business transactions' with the institutions where the research is being done	Ring binder
Research proposal and correspondence about it with the institution	Ring binder
Action plans/timetables	Visual display
Your own development of ideas; research maps; 'diary notes'; reminders of things to follow up	Word-processed files and printout
	Notebooks
Correspondence about the research	Ring binder(s)
Documents designed for use in the research, eg questionnaires, standard letters	Ring binder(s) word-processed file
Decisions about 'house style'	Word-processed file and printout
Contacts	Card index (hard copy or on computer)

Table 4.1   Appropriate forms of storage for documentation.

Two pieces of useful advice about storing documentation:

1 *Date everything you keep!*
2 Keep a notebook or a file for thoughts that suddenly present themselves, and ideas about things to follow up.

Using the documentation

Make a regular appointment with yourself to review what's been going on recently. Sit down with the results of whatever you've been doing, together with the relevant formal documents.

The very fact of bringing together the range of things you have been doing, and thinking about them in relation to one another, allows them to interact creatively. It is like a meeting of people who are working away separately at their own bits of a project, at which they can exchange news and negotiate useful joint action.

More than that, doing something practical, where you can put your thoughts outside in the world and actually see them, relieves the stress of having it all inside the head. And if you have a session of doing nothing more than sorting documents and putting them into tidy containers, that in itself has a calming and organizing effect on the mind at times when you feel under too much pressure to do anything more demanding.

A checklist of questions to ask at a review session:

- Have I acted on all the points arising from the last session?
- Am I up to schedule? If not, what action can I take to improve the situation?
- What have I done since last time?
- What are the key things I've learned?
- How do they affect the assumptions I started with?

When you have had a review session, record the results. Keep them where you will see them, and act on them. At the next session, start by checking the actions taken.

Use such documents as questionnaire formats and test record ing forms in the final product of the research, as examples to show how you have done the things you report on (see Chapter 7, page 111).

Use your records of changes and developments, and your own ideas about the criteria that should be applied in assessing your work, in preparing for the oral examination or interview with the examiners.

5 | Managing the time available

Alice sighed wearily. 'I think you might do something better with the time,' she said, 'than waste it in asking riddles that have no answers.'

'If you knew Time as well as I do,' said the Hatter, 'you wouldn't talk about wasting it. It's him.'

'I don't know what you mean,' said Alice.

'Of course you don't!' the Hatter said ... 'I dare say you never even spoke to Time!'

'Perhaps not,' Alice cautiously replied; 'but I know I have to beat time when I learn music.'

'Ah! That accounts for it,' said the Hatter. 'He won't stand beating. Now, if you only kept on good terms with him, he'd do almost anything you liked with the clock. ...'

(LEWIS CARROLL, *Alice's Adventures in Wonderland*, 1865,
Chapter 7)

Research – particularly in its last stages, when everything has to be brought together and submitted by a due date – is notoriously a stressful business, and few of us get through it without experiencing moments of despair, panic, acute anxiety, rage, or tears. Getting things done to time is a major contributor to the stress; and it has sometimes seemed to me that some researchers actually put time obstacles in their own way, as if in their hearts they do not think themselves worthy to succeed. Often it is the people who have most potential to deliver excellent work who suffer in this way, and it is painful to watch their struggles. Others are just unrealistically optimistic about what they can do at the eleventh hour, and most have never had the opportunity of developing the straightforward skills that at least help us to plan good productive use of time. So this chapter sets out some quite simple everyday ways by which researchers can help themselves to:
- Create realistic schedules
- Plan sensible sequences of activities
- Deal with slippages
- Enhance their speed of working without sacrificing quality.

Since the advice and the messages are quite straightforward ones, and since I am trying to help readers to save time, the presentation in this chapter is designed as far as possible to save reading time without reducing understanding. It covers:

- Questions that help us to treat time well
- Scheduling
- What to do if you can't keep to your time commitments
- Timesavers.

Questions that help us to treat time well

Here again, I would like to invite readers to answer the questions in relation to their own projects. The very process of setting down the facts about what we have to do, and the time constraints within which we have to do it – even when they are quite well known to us (and they aren't always!) – helps us to see a way forward, and can remove some of the sense of oppression and anxiety about getting it all done in time that usually accompanies research.

WHAT ARE THE MOST IMPORTANT THINGS I HAVE TO DO?
Making a straightforward list of things that have to be done is as useful in research as in daily life; it takes one burden from memory, and allows us to inspect the tasks that lie ahead and make some decisions.

> **Example 1**
> A project on 'integrated pest management' (the research project presented in Chapter 2, pages 22 to 25)

1 Locate and read the relevant literature.
2 Draw on experience of staff members who have relevant consultancy experience in developing countries.
3 Gather information on pesticide use and knowledge of economic thresholds in East Anglia: (a) discussions with Agricultural Development and Advisory Service; (b) discussions with National Farmers Union; and (c) questionnaire and interviews with sample of farmers.
4 Analyse findings from questionnaire and interviews.
5 Draw conclusions and suggest appropriate action for:
   (a) East Anglia; and (b) developing countries.
6 Write report on project.

   ○ END OF EXAMPLE I

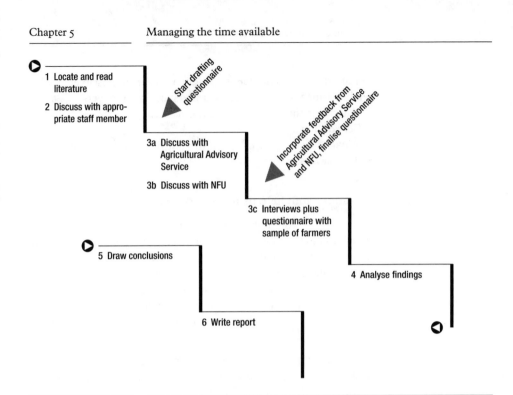

Figure 5.1   Sequence of research activities.

HOW DO THE THINGS I HAVE TO DO DEPEND ON EACH
OTHER? WHAT ORDER MUST I DO THEM IN?
A list of tasks makes it easy to see which ones have to be done before others can be started, and which can run side by side.

> **Example 2**
> Example 1 continued (see Figure 5.1 above)

1 and 2 can run side by side.

3a and 3b can come in when 1 and 2 are sufficiently advanced for me to have clear ideas for discussion.

3c will depend on what I learn from 1, 2, and 3a and 3b, but I can start drafting the questionnaire at the end of 2, and get feedback on it from discussions of 3a and 3b.

4 depends on 3.

5 depends on 4.

6 depends on 5.

◉ END OF EXAMPLE 2

WHAT ARE THE DEADLINES?

In a research project, there are always deadlines at which specific things have to be delivered, and 'milestones' on the way towards the final fateful date on which the fruits of the research have to be delivered up to judgement. If the language of the last sentence sounds apocalyptic, remember that the best way of making the actual business less like the end of the world is to confront the deadlines squarely, and to know exactly what you have to do by what time. I have often been surprised and troubled by students' lack of knowledge of the times at which their course requires that various things be done. Simple self-preservation requires that you should have this knowledge, and if it has not been given to you, then ask until you get a satisfactory answer.

When you get the necessary information, sort it out into chronological order, and make it into a visual display which shows you at a glance the deadlines you have to meet and the milestones on the way. The next example suggests one way of doing this.

| **Example 3**
| A research programme leading to an MA

I choose this example because I have found from experience that students on this programme are often unaware of the sequence of events, the things they are required to do, and the dates by which they are supposed to do them. They have a student handbook which actually contains the necessary information – but so embedded in a complex text that it is difficult to disentangle it. Once it is extracted, it can be organized into a simple display of key dates and activities, as shown in Figures 5.2 and 5.3 on pages 78 and 79.

O END OF EXAMPLE 3

HOW LONG CAN I AFFORD TO TAKE?

Work it out in relation to other activities which will require your time, like lectures, workshops, laboratory or studio work, or, if you are doing your research part-time, the demands of your regular occupation. Allow for thinking time – if you try to do things without having thought properly about them, they take longer and the results aren't satisfactory.

02 – 06 08:	**Pre-course summer school**
Week beginning	**Term 1**
11 10	2-day project
18 10	Deliver report on project
25 10	Prepare material for termly progress review
15 11	Termly progress review
Week beginning	**Term 2**
26 01	Prepare seminar presentation for next week
02 02	Presentations on seminar topics to student group
09 02	2-day project
16 02	Deliver report on project
23 02	Prepare material for termly progress review
02 03	Termly progress review
09 03	Prepare preliminary Statement of Intent
20 – 22 03	Weekend school on research methodology
Week beginning	**Term 3**
13 04	Statement of Intent (final version)
20 04	Prepare presentation on MA project
04 05	Presentations on MA projects
11 05	Meeting with external Assessor
18 05	Discuss draft of dissertation with tutors
25 05	Discuss draft of critical appraisal with tutors
Week beginning	**Term 4**
21 09	Start preparing draft Assessment Contract
12 10	Deliver final version of Assessment Contract
09 11	Hand in dissertation and critical appraisal
08 12	Final examination

Figure 5.2   Key dates and activities.

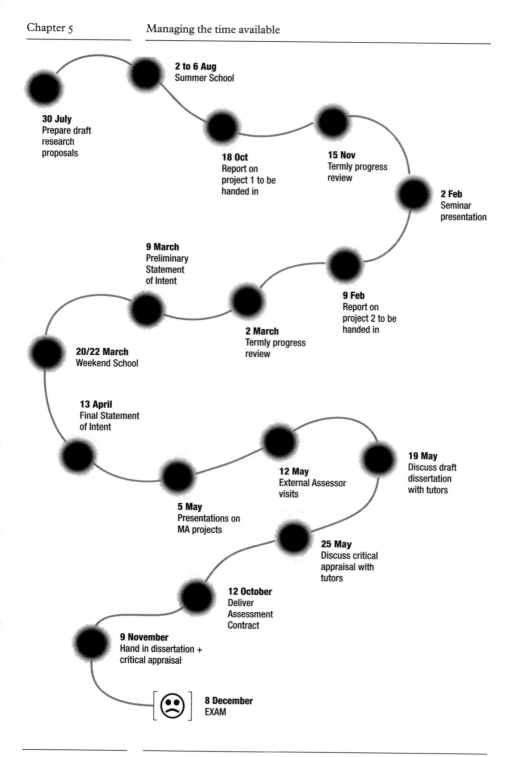

30 July
Prepare draft
research
proposals

2 to 6 Aug
Summer School

18 Oct
Report on
project 1 to be
handed in

15 Nov
Termly progress
review

2 Feb
Seminar
presentation

9 March
Preliminary
Statement
of Intent

9 Feb
Report on
project 2 to be
handed in

2 March
Termly progress
review

20/22 March
Weekend School

13 April
Final Statement
of Intent

12 May
External Assessor
visits

19 May
Discuss draft
dissertation
with tutors

5 May
Presentations on
MA projects

25 May
Discuss critical
appraisal with
tutors

12 October
Deliver
Assessment
Contract

9 November
Hand in dissertation +
critical appraisal

8 December
EXAM

Figure 5.3　　　An alternative way of showing key dates and activities.

| **Example 4**
| Based on Example 3

This example takes two of the activities that have to be completed by a deadline, and shows the factors that have to be taken into account in deciding how much time can be spent on them and when it should be spent.

Term 3

1 MA Statement of Intent (final version) – to be presented at start of term.
2 Presentations of MA projects to tutors and fellow-students.

1 MA Statement of Intent (final version)
Based on the first version, done in term 1, and has to be ready for start of term 3. So do it during vacation between terms 2 & 3.
   Other things going on then:
• Reading on MA topic
• Planning practical work
• Planning dissertation outline.
Implications for planning:
Given that it's based on first version, and needs to draw on reading and planning, better plan to do it late in vacation, to allow for thinking time. Allow 2 days for drafting and editing into final version, in last week of vacation.

2 Presentation of MA projects
Presentations come towards end of term 3. They entail:
• Preparing a talk (something unfamiliar to many people, so allow plenty of preparation and rehearsal time), and visuals to illustrate it.
Sources:
• Reading, notes, etc. towards MA project
• Anything relevant done in terms 1 & 2.
   Other things going on then :
• Research
• Practical work of various kinds
• Student-led group discussions
• Starting to work on assessment contract
• Drafting dissertation and planning critical evaluation.
Implications for planning:
• Start planning in fortnight before half-term

- Feed relevant material from reading, practical work, etc. into framework
- Devote a week to it just after half-term, with as few other activities as possible
- One day to polish and rehearse in week before presentations.
- If possible, plan presentation so that it can be used as basis for a chapter in dissertation.

    ○ END OF EXAMPLE 4

Things that take longer than you may imagine:
- Writing: for most of us it is a slow and tiring process, though there are ways of overcoming some of the difficulties (see Chapters 7 and 8).
- Transcribing and editing from tape recordings: if research involves interviewing people or meetings, it is a temptation to think that recording the proceedings will save time and trouble. It won't; even if you can type quickly, transcription is a laborious business, and you are still left with the job of editing the text down to what you need for your purposes.
- Preparing diagrams and tables: even when you have set standards for their presentation (see Chapter 9), they still demand a lot of time and care if they are to be produced to a respectable standard.
- Final checking and editing: examiners are rightly upset by such things as lack of pagination, a contents list which does not correspond with the actual contents, erratic spelling and punctuation, incorrect versions of authors' names, incomplete references, inconsistent statements, and sentences that come unstuck in the middle. Cleaning up the final product so that it is free of distracting blemishes is not a quick job. I recently edited a thesis for a colleague; it had been meticulously prepared in many ways, but it still took me 25 hours of quite intensive work. So allow something like one working day per chapter for this kind of checking.

HOW CAN I ESTIMATE HOW LONG THINGS WILL TAKE?
Working out how long you can allow yourself for a particular task is one thing. Knowing whether you can complete it in the time is another. Being able to estimate how long a given job will take is an essential survival skill, and it can usually be learned by practice. Those who don't acquire it are liable to find themselves working for more hours than they bargained for on tasks, and

consequently being paid less, or they disappoint people for whom they work and get a reputation for unreliability.

Some ways of finding out how long key research activities actually take
Time yourself on sample tasks, such as:
- Reading a typical ten-page article in your subject area and making brief notes on it
- Planning a chapter
- Carrying out an interview and inputting the notes from it.

If you plan to use a questionnaire or to carry out a series of tests:
- Try out the questions or the test instructions first to make sure they are clear and unambiguous to the kind of people who will be responding.
- Time how long it takes to prepare the responses for analysis.

WHAT DO I DO IF AN ESSENTIAL ACTIVITY IS GOING TO TAKE MORE TIME THAN I CAN AFFORD?
If it really is an essential activity, without which you cannot achieve what you undertook to do in the research, you either have to find ways of doing it more efficiently or to save the necessary time on other activities. These questions may help:
- Are there alternative ways of doing it that would take less time, for example a short structured interview rather than a lengthy questionnaire, or reducing the sample size for a series of tests?
- Can you reduce or cut out some other activity? (If you do that, the research map may need some redrawing, and you will probably need to notify your tutors.)
- Can you speed up your performance, for example by learning how to touch-type, or by doing a short course on study skills?

WHOM ELSE DO I DEPEND ON FOR MEETING DEADLINES?
It's seldom the case that a research project is dependent on the efforts of the researcher alone. If interviews or visits to organizations are a part of the research, you will be dependent on the goodwill and availability of the people you wish to see; if you want to carry out tests involving other people, you have to get your subjects together at a convenient time and place; if you need access to computing facilities or specialist equipment, so do many others whose claim is equal to yours; print rooms and reprographic departments have to serve whole institutions, and their equipment is not immune from breakdown.

Other people's priorities are different from yours!
Plan ahead and make your arrangements in good time.

Scheduling

When you know the key deadlines and have worked out when major tasks have to be done (see pages 77 to 81), and how long they will take, it's a good idea to make a detailed schedule for the period immediately ahead, so that you can see what you propose to be doing with your time. Having it displayed makes it easier to monitor how you are using the available time; you can tick off things as you do them, which is encouraging; and you can show changes in sequence if you have to amend your schedule. Figure 5.4 on page 84 shows some methods of displaying a schedule.

What to do if you can't keep to your time commitments

Sometimes it's impossible to keep to a schedule. The cause may lie wholly outside the control of the researcher, it may be partly external and partly subjective, or it may be wholly subjective.

EXTERNAL CAUSES

If you are thwarted from doing one thing on your schedule because, for example, an appointment has to be rescheduled, use the time you had set aside for it for something else. Never do nothing! There should always be ongoing activities such as reading, reviewing progress, sorting out notes, or drafting, which can be brought forward to fill gaps.

CAUSES THAT LIE PARTLY OR WHOLLY WITHIN THE RESEARCHER

Researchers' timetables can get seriously set back because of a combination of externally originating obstacles and their own physical or mental state. If you can't get at a computer when you need to, or an essential book you had reserved doesn't come in when you need it, and on top of that the current virus strikes you down for a week, things will inevitably slip, and you are more than likely to feel unable to cope with the situation.

If something like this happens, don't try to struggle on in the face of illness. Let your tutors know, and concentrate on getting better. When you feel more like a human being, you will be able to reschedule and continue. If it's a prolonged illness at a critical time, your institution will have arrangements for an extension of time to make up for the time lost. If you just feel frustrated, fed

[83]

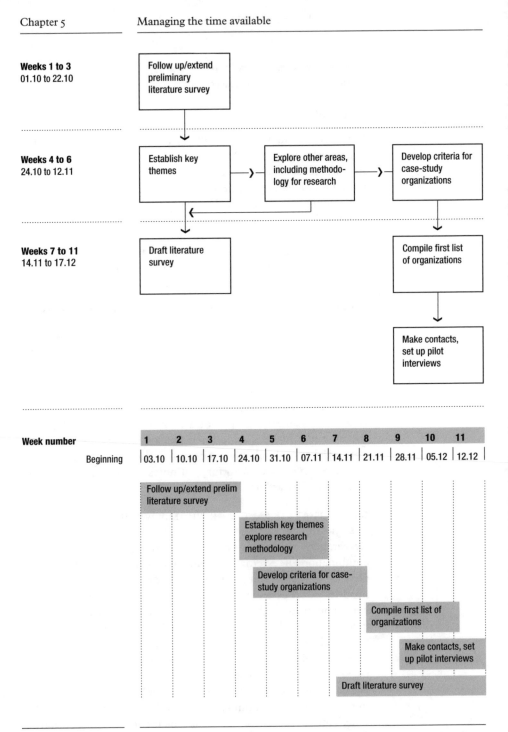

up, and not quite yourself, take it as a signal that you should pause for a while – I find that going for a quiet walk helps to restore equilibrium, and the rhythm of walking often promotes the sorting out of tangled thoughts.

Should you find that, without actual physical illness or external frustrations, you are getting seriously behind on your schedule, don't pretend to anybody – least of all yourself – that all is well; don't feel ashamed that you can't keep up; and don't keep the trouble to yourself. Tell your tutors, take advantage of your college's provisions for pastoral help or counselling if you feel they would help. Research can be a lonely occupation, especially if it's the first time you have done it, and if you have not previously had to take responsibility for managing your own work it can be daunting. You should know that you are not alone in this – many researchers suffer in this way. Being able to talk it through with others, who understand something about both your project and the anxieties of researchers, should help you to work out a new approach to the research which will allow you to get to grips with it and to make friends again with time.

Timesavers

This is my personal list of timesavers – the steps which I have found from many years of experience (having started off as a rather disorganized and untidy research student) actually save time for me. They may not do the trick for everyone – we all have a different approach to work, and what helps me may look like self-imposed torment and a serious hindrance to others. The main thing is to be aware of your own natural ways of working – what makes you feel at ease, what constrains you and makes you unhappy. Then look for improvements that can support you in working in ways that you find comfortable, and can save you time. They may involve a small element of self-discipline, but once you find something that pays off, the necessary self-discipline stops being a burden and becomes an unnoticed part of your way of working.

- Interleave your activities
- Run different tasks concurrently, not end-on – in other words, don't just do one thing at a time! Alternate between different jobs so that you are going forward on two or more fronts at once – Example 2, earlier in this Chapter (page 76) shows an example of a researcher deciding which activities can run side by side.

– Don't spend too long at a time on things that demand intense concentration and sitting in one place. Start in good time on the demanding ones (especially writing) and break them into short sessions, with different and less demanding activities in between. Don't be deluded by what our family doctor used to call 'fatigue fever' – the condition that sets in when you force yourself to go on working past the time when your stamina and concentration have declined. The work that results will be flawed, and you will be no good for some time to come. As an editor of other people's writing, I can spot when they have pushed themselves to go on after the point when they were too fatigued to do the job properly.

• Find out what time of day is your best working time, and do the things that demand most concentration and creative thought then – whether it's early morning or late at night.

• Keep everything relating to your research in good order, so that you don't waste time looking for particular sets of notes, or the phone numbers of essential contacts.

• Invest time (as suggested in Chapter 3) in giving yourself tools to help you to find relevant material among what you have collected. The single step that has saved me most time and contributed most to making my work effective was setting up a database into which I input every article I find that contains useful information.

• Before starting on any job, assemble everything you need for it.

• When you've finished a session of note-taking – from reading, from meetings with people, or from lectures – highlight the key points in the notes while your memory is still fresh. It saves time later, when you need to use the notes as the basis for writing.

• 'When found, make a note of.' Follow the advice of Dickens's Captain Cuttle *(Dombey and Son)*. Always make an immediate note of good ideas that come to you, and of things you suddenly realize you ought to do, etc., so that you don't lose them and then have to waste time trying to remember what it was you thought of.

• Learn to touch-type, reasonably quickly and accurately, using all the fingers that nature has given you. If you can do that, you will be typing three times faster than you would if you were pecking at the keyboard with two fingers. You will also find it less fatiguing, because you will be able to keep looking at what you are typing from (or even to shut your eyes if you are composing out of your head), rather than shuttling your gaze back and forth from copy to keys.

- Avoid copy-typing. I have met students who actually wrote their whole dissertation in longhand, and then laboriously copy-typed it. That's a sad waste of time and effort. If you transcribe from one form to another – say from handwritten notes to a word-processed file – always add value in the process. Reorganize the notes into a form that brings significant material together and emphasizes the key points, so that you have a piece of text which is easy to use as the basis for drafting a chapter. Or even practise marking up and coding your handwritten notes so that you can go direct from them to a draft (see Figures 10.4 and 10.5 on pages 169 and 170).

- At the end of each session of writing, put a note at the point where you stopped, to remind yourself what to do next, so that you see it as soon as you return to the job. It helps to save the time that otherwise goes on wondering 'What on earth was I doing? Did I really write that? What did I mean to say next?'

6 | Planning the information products of research: questions to answer

Researchers have to transform the results of their research into a variety of primary and secondary 'information products'.[1] The first thing their institution will require of them will be called by various names: research report, major project report, dissertation, thesis; some institutions also ask for supplementary products, such as 'evaluative reports', 'research diaries' and 'executive summaries'. Later, the research may well form the basis for articles, books, educational texts or conference papers. Some researchers may also be under an obligation to present a report on their research to the organizations which employ them and have sponsored their studies. Each different product has its own audience, and each audience has its own needs. It is the obligation of the researcher to transform the knowledge which he/she has gained from research into an information product appropriate for its intended users. Meeting the obligation demands hard thinking, but brings great satisfaction when we know that we have made something from our research which will help its readers to gain the understanding they need.

This chapter will suggest a series of questions that researchers need to ask and answer – about the readers who will use the products of their research, the ways in which they will want to use it, their expectations in reading, the constraints and requirements that have to be met in creating and delivering the products, and about the research itself.

This chapter will suggest a series of questions that researchers need to ask and answer – about the readers who will use the products of their research, the ways in which they will want to use it, their expectations in reading, the constraints and requirements

---

[1] 'Information product' is a term that has come into use over the last few years to describe the products (print on paper or electronic) that are designed to convey specific information to meet the needs of particular groups of users. Besides the reports, dissertations, etc. resulting from research, other examples of information products include: reference books, instruction manuals or brochures for products, timetables, textbooks and handbooks.

that have to be met in creating and delivering the products, and about the research itself.

The answers, when put together and considered as a whole, can act as a reliable indicator when we come to make decisions about how to present the research in the required products.[2]

They will help in making decisions on such features as:
- Structure
- Content and emphasis
- Choice of words, style of writing, and visual methods of presentation
- Level of presentation
- Size, shape, binding
- Time management

At the end of this chapter, the suggested questions are set out in the form of a checklist, which you may like to use in your own planning, in conjunction with reading Chapter 7, which deals with using the answers to make the decisions.

The right time to start planning

Thinking about the end product of research is not something to be left until a final writing stage a short time before the report or dissertation is due to be delivered. It is best to regard it as a basic repeated process, a cycle that you go round several times during the development of the research and your thinking about it. If you do that, the final product will become a part of your thinking, and ideas about it will take shape organically as the research proceeds, instead of having to be crudely hammered out at the last moment. Initially, it may not be possible to answer all the questions, and to some you may be able only to give a provisional answer, but that in itself will focus attention on things you still have to find out which have an important bearing on the final product.

The users of the research

The first questions concern the people who will read and use the products of the research for various purposes. For each kind of

---

[2] This process of asking questions and drawing implications from them is, by the way, a characteristic 'design approach' used by typographic designers in planning the visual presentation of printed information; asking the right questions about a design problem is an important stage in the process before designing actually starts.

research product that we have to create, we need to define who
the users are, how they will wish to use the products we give
them, what their purposes will be in reading them and what they
will be looking to find in them.

WHO ARE THE USERS?
- Who is going to read and use the product?

One person? Many people? Will it be read by one particular
group of people with a similar background, or by people from
many different backgrounds? Will it be read initially by a small
group of people who have to make a judgement on it, and later
on by other researchers in search of information relevant to their
own work? If it will be read by two very different groups, for example academics and managers in an organization which has
sponsored the research, can the requirements of both be met by a
single product?

- What do they know about the subject of the research?

Are they experts? Do they have a general knowledge of the
broad topic, but not specific knowledge of the detailed research
area? Is it outside their present experience, but something which
is potentially important for them?

Different levels of knowledge require different approaches to
writing (see Chapter 8 for more on meeting the requirement). In
writing dissertations or research reports it's particularly important to give examiners credit for being knowledgeable in the field
of the research – treating them to well-worn quotations from
standard textbooks, for instance, is not an infallible way to their
hearts.

- What is their relation to the research and to you as the researcher?

Have they been associated with it from the start? Did they
commission or sponsor it? Did they set the brief for it? Or will the
report or dissertation or article be their first meeting with it?

The answers will help in deciding how much background explanation is necessary to enable the users to orient themselves,
what knowledge you can safely assume, and what is the appropriate tone of writing.

FOR WHAT PURPOSES WILL THEY WANT TO USE
THE PRODUCT?
- As an element in their evaluation of your performance in the
  research? As the basis for taking decisions on action (this is likely

to be the case if the research has been sponsored or commissioned)? To learn something relevant to their own work?

- And how will they want to use it? Will they read it from start to finish? Or will they want to form an overall idea of what it's about, and to 'sample' it as part of the process of assessing a group of products when there is not time to read them in detail? (this does happen; see pages 92–93 for advice on finding out what you need to know for self-preservation about your institution's examining procedures). Will they want to look up specific pieces of information? Or will they be seeking to understand particular concepts? Or to learn how to carry out processes?

WHAT FORM OF PRESENTATION ARE THEY USED TO?
Highly 'traditional' academic dissertations (the kind where the researcher must never under any circumstances say 'I did this ...' but always 'This was done to ...')? Scientific periodical articles? The professional, trade or technical press in their own field? Technical reports? Reports to management? Government publications?

Asking people – particularly those whose judgements will affect our future – to cope with products which are very different in form, structure or language from the ones they are accustomed to reading can be a dangerous undertaking. On the other hand, if the content you have to convey does not fit easily into the forms your readers are most accustomed to, you are entitled to seek another form which does the job so much better than the traditional one that readers will appreciate the benefits (see Chapter 9).

Setting your own agenda

So much for the users of the information products of research. Less obviously, perhaps, but equally important, we have to define our own relationship with the readers, and to express to ourselves what *we* seek from that silent encounter with them which takes place through the medium of what we have written. It is important to be aware of the power for influencing readers' judgement and feelings that the writer can exercise – simply by virtue of the concentrated and structured knowledge that he/she builds up in the process of research – and to set our own 'agenda' for the outcomes of the meeting with the readers. So we need to ask ourselves:

- What do *I* want to get out of this?
- What do I most want my readers to understand?

- What do I want them to think and to feel as a result of reading what I have written?
- How do I want them to think of me?

There is self-presentation of the writer even in the most impersonal and constrained forms of writing, and it is worth pausing to consider how we ourselves as readers respond to what comes across to us of the writer. For myself, in the course of some years as a technical book editor, I came to recognize many different qualities in the writers whose work I subbed – authority and integrity based on deep knowledge and meticulous checking; wit that emerged slyly in impeccably academic writing; clarity of mind in the management of arguments. Sometimes, alas, less admirable traits revealed themselves – lack of thorough understanding of concepts, revealed by tangled syntax; carelessness in verification, which made it essential to double-check for consistency between text and the numbers in tables; and just occasionally a smirking self-regard which was rather greater than the self in question merited.

Constraints and requirements

In beginning any piece of work, it is an essential piece of self-preservation to know the things we *must* do, and the *limits* within which we have to operate. And it should not be regarded as just a tiresome restriction – understanding necessity in the form of the constraints within which we have to act is essential for defining the degree of freedom which we enjoy, and a stimulus for making good and ingenious use of it. So we need to ask:

- When does the product have to be presented?
- What are the existing standards of presentation?

There may be certain features that must be present, while there may also be some latitude in other matters. Consult your supervisor, get hold of any written rules, and look at a range of existing products that have been submitted for the degree in order to identify ways of presentation that could be useful – and those which make life difficult for the reader!

- What form of technology for production is available? (for example, word-processing, desktop publishing).

Is it mandatory? Does prescribed software have to be used? Are there limits on the typefaces that can be used? Is there a house style that has to be observed? And are there limits on access to the technology – for example, are the computers used for teaching on certain days and not available for work on dissertations? Is there access at weekends and in the evenings?

- How many copies of dissertations or reports are required? Who has to receive copies?
  The answers to these questions are essential for decisions on:
- Production methods
- Materials
- Time management (especially if we are dependent for production on other people with many schedules to meet).

Other people with an interest

It is your responsibility, at an early stage in your research, to study and understand the rules for assessment for the course you are taking. Different institutions, and different schools within the same institution, have different procedures for assessment, and you need to know from the beginning how many people will examine your work; how internal and external assessments take place; and who is involved in them.

- To whom are you answerable on presentation of the research?
- Who has to approve your decisions?
- Whose co-operation do you need in presenting the research? For example: subject specialists in other locations; computer staff; keyboard operators.
- What specialist facilities do you need to use?
- Do you need to learn any new techniques or methods in order to carry through your research?
  The answers are particularly critical for time management, because if we need the help and goodwill of other people, we have to set aside time for negotiating with them, as well as for their giving us the co-operation we seek; and their priorities will be different from ours, so they can't be relied on to be able to give immediate attention to what we want.

The research itself

Finally, we need to ask questions about the nature of the research itself, and here, above all, reiterating the questions at intervals will yield valuable insights into what form the end product should take. Chapter 4 referred to the benefits of redrawing and updating the research map; one of the chief benefits is being able to think consistently about what the evolving map implies for the presentation of the information products of the research. For the first time round, the starting point will be the initial statement of research objectives or the research proposal; as the work goes forward and the documentation develops it should be possible to set key stages for repeating these questions:

- What is the purpose of the research?

  Has it changed since the first statement? If it has, what has led to the modification?

- How is it being carried out?

  What are the key features of the methodology? Is it experiment-based? Does it rely on quantitative data gathering? Or is it essentially qualitative? Does it use questionnaires or interviews? Is it based on the researcher's participation in some form of action research? Has it evolved in new directions different from the methods first proposed?

- What are the key findings so far?

  What light do they throw on the original assumptions? Are there any significant ones which were unexpected? What conclusions do they seem to point to?

- How do you yourself evaluate the work you have done so far?

  Is it achieving what it set out to do? Is there anything you did not anticipate, but which you now realize you should have anticipated? Are the methods you chose appropriate? What is the most useful result or finding so far?

- What are the most important things that you want readers of the research product to understand about the research?
- How do you envisage it could be used? How might it be followed up?

  The answers to these questions will contribute to decisions about:
- Structure
- Content
- What we emphasize
- How we distribute data between main text and appendices
- Choice of visual presentation to match the nature of data, to make structures and connections clear, arguments easy to follow, etc.

  All the questions that have been suggested in this chapter have been brought together into a checklist, which appears below. You may like to try answering the questions for whatever stage of research you yourself have reached, before going on to Chapter 7, so that you can see how it works as an aid to making decisions about research products.

Checklist

THE USERS
1 Who will read and use the research product?
2 What do they know about the subject of the research?
3 What is their relation to the research?
4 For what purposes will they use the research product?
5 How will they want to use it?
6 What form of presentation are they used to?
   Making use of the answers to these questions: see Chapters 7 & 8.

YOUR OWN AGENDA
7 What do I want to get out of this for myself?
8 What do I most want my readers to understand?
9 What do I want them to think and feel as a result of reading?
10 How do I want them to think of me?
   Making use of the answers to these questions: see Chapters 7 & 8.

CONSTRAINTS AND REQUIREMENTS
11 When does the product have to be presented?
   For meeting the time constraints: see Chapter 5
12 What are the existing standards of presentation?
13 What form of technology is available for production?
14 Do I have to use any particular form of technology?
15 Are there any constraints in the way I have to use the technology?
16 How many copies of the product are required?
17 To whom do they have to be delivered?
   Making use of the answers to these questions: see Chapter 9.

OTHER PEOPLE WITH AN INTEREST
18 To whom am I answerable on presentation of the research?
19 Who has to approve my decisions?
20 Whose co-operation do I need?
21 What specialist facilities do I need to use?
22 What things do I need to learn?
   See Chapter 5 for the time-management aspect of these questions.

THE RESEARCH

23 What is the purpose of the research?
    See Chapter 2 for examples of first definition of research purposes.
24 Has it changed in the course of the research? Why?
25 How is it being carried out?
26 What are the key findings so far?
27 How do I evaluate the work done so far?
28 What are the most important things that I want readers to understand?
29 How might the research be used? What useful contribution could it make? How might it be followed up?
30 Is the research product a
    Dissertation/thesis?
    Research report?
    Project report?
    Article?
    Something else?
    Making use of the answers to these questions: see Chapters 7 to 10.

7 | Planning the information products of research: first decisions

The last chapter presented questions that researchers need to ask themselves about:

- The research itself
- The users of the research product and the ways in which they will want to use it
- The obligations we have to meet in presenting the product; the things we must do, may do, and must not on any account do.

Our answers to these questions in effect identify the 'market' for the product of the research, and the constraints and requirements that it has to meet. This chapter is about looking at the implications of our answers, and, on the basis of them, making some first decisions about the 'shape' of the end product. Those decisions in turn will point us towards more detailed ones, which will ultimately help us to define the content, form and qualities of the final product that we create and present.

The decisions are, as Figure 7.1 shows (see page 98), all interrelated, and they have to take into account the interrelation of the answers to the original questions, and that is not always easy, because an ideal solution to one aspect may not be so good for another. (For example, some parts of a project report may be best handled by straightforward prose narrative, while other parts may require very little text but a lot of tables and diagrams; a page layout that would work well for the plain prose text might make it very difficult to place the tables and diagrams so that readers could easily relate them to the text that belongs with them.)

Figure 7.2 (see page 99) shows the kind of process we need to go through to arrive at sensible decisions – a repeated cycle of asking and answering questions, analysing the answers, making decisions, asking and answering more questions, and so on, until we arrive at a final set of decisions that takes into account all the answers to all the questions.

This chapter looks particularly at the answers to the questions about the users, the researcher's own agenda, and the research itself, and at what the answers imply for the character of the final product. Once again, I have tried to combine general advice with examples drawn from actual research.

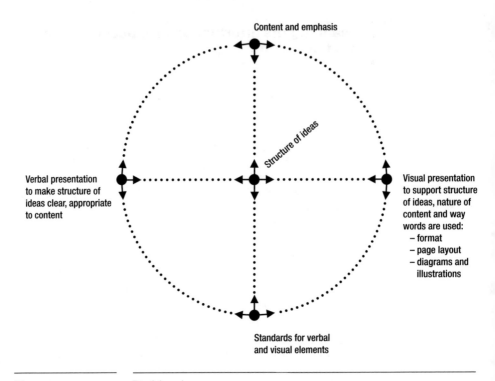

Figure 7.1   Decisions interact.

The users

WHAT DO USERS NEED?

All users need to be able to see what the product is about, and to find their way into it and around it with the minimum of obstacles and with the maximum of help from the author.

The people who have to evaluate and assess the product need to be able to:
- Understand what the research aims to do
- Appreciate the reasons for the choice of methods
- Follow and check the reasoning
- See what the conclusions are, and find the evidence for them.

These are also the main needs of sponsors in dealing with a report based on the research. They may well also be looking for:
- Recommendations for action, and the case for taking it.

The people who will want to use research products to find useful information for their own purposes need to:
- Find the information relevant to their needs

[98]

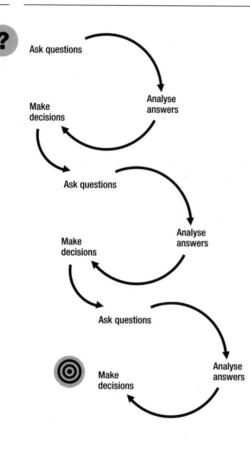

| **Figure 7.2** | The process of arriving at decisions. |

- See the relationships between the different parts of it
- Match up the information with what they already know
- Turn the information into usable knowledge.

And they want to do all that as quickly and with as little trouble as possible. Now let us relate those general requirements to a particular case.

| **Example 1**
| A specific research project

The project is the one described in Chapter 2 (see pages 28 – 33): 'The role of information products and information presentation in organizations'. The research topics include: what organizations do at present in the way of presenting information for internal use, and for communication with their 'outside world'; whether they have any specific strategy for what they do in this respect; how they take their decisions; the people who create the products; and technologies they use. Because of the nature of the project, the main work rests on case studies and action research in a range of organizations of various kinds.

The questions about the users (from the checklist in Chapter 6, pages 95 and 96), and the answers for this research

1 Who will read and use the research product?
2 What do they know about the subject of the research?
3 What is their relation to the research?
4 For what purposes will they use the research product?
5 How will they want to use it?
6 What form of presentation are they used to?

Three sets of users are concerned here: the examiners who will assess the final thesis; the managers of the case study organizations, who will read and comment on the case study reports before I finalize them; and readers with an interest in the area of the research who will read the thesis for their own purposes.

THE EXAMINERS

The research area is on the borders between various disciplines, and the examiners will bring specialist knowledge to some of the topics, but may not be well acquainted with others. So I shall have to pay particular attention to the unfamiliar areas, without making the necessary explanations look like teaching grandmother to suck eggs. This will apply particularly to establishing what the research aims to do and why it is relevant, and to aspects concerned with information design.

I suspect that the form of presentation they are used to is the conventional thesis, with an impersonal style of writing, using passive rather than active verbs, a fair amount of specialized terminology, and an emphasis on continuous text. The nature of the material I shall want to present implies a rather different approach, with a good deal of example material and graphical treatment. And the fact that the research is largely based on case studies means that a great deal depends on personal interaction between researcher and individuals in the organizations – which can't be conveyed in traditional 'third person' terms. The implication is that I shall need to prepare my ground carefully beforehand, to ensure that the way I present the thesis does not come as a shock to the system. So, plenty of discussion with my supervisor, showing examples of possible ways of presentation from an early stage; and a careful introduction to the thesis itself, making clear the reasons for departures from convention, in terms of the nature of the material itself, and of making it accessible to users. I have to convince the examiners that while it may look different from what they are used to, there is a good reason for the difference, and I haven't sacrificed academic rigour.

THE MANAGERS OF THE CASE STUDY ORGANIZATIONS
It's part of the deal with case study organizations that in return for access and people's time, I will provide them with a draft report to management, covering my findings and conclusions on the topics investigated in the case study. It's worth doing this, because the reports presented to managements will form the basis for how I present the case studies in the thesis, and the response to them will yield useful additional material. The reports can be structured around the topics discussed in the organizations (a checklist is given to everyone concerned beforehand, and we use it as a framework in the interviews), and they will fit quite comfortably into a fairly conventional report format, though, as explained above, the style will not be too impersonal. The difficult bit will be how I provide comments on the actual examples of their publications. I think the way to deal with this will be to take a small but representative sample, and to apply a set of tests to each item, something like this, perhaps:

1 The role of the product:
- What is the purpose of this product in relation to the organization's objectives?
- How are its readers meant to use it?

2 The information elements in the product.

3 How it meets its purpose:
- Does it tell the readers what they need to know in order to use it as intended?

- Does it give them:
- The right amount of detail?
- Too much?
- Too little?

- Does it present information in a sequence which:
- Makes it accessible?

- Facilitates understanding?
- Helps readers to act as intended?

• Does the presentation match the experience and expectations of readers in respect of:
- Vocabulary?
- Sentence structure?
- Numerical data?
- Graphics?

• Does the typography support the ways in which readers need to use the product, in respect of:
- Legibility/readability?
- Use of spacing as an aid to comprehension?
- Choice of format?
- Measure?
- Choice of typeface?
- Consistency of treatment of information elements?
- Making the structure of the product clear?
- Guiding readers through the sequence in which information is presented?

• Does the method of reproduction meet the purposes of the product and the needs of the readers?

• Are the materials appropriate for the purposes of the product and the needs of the readers?

OTHER READERS WITH AN INTEREST IN THE AREA
If I can meet the requirements of the examiners and the managers, in the way outlined above, then I've cracked it for the other readers too.

◉ END OF EXAMPLE I

The researcher's own agenda

For most of us, doing research is one of the few occasions when we are responsible for all the decisions about a piece of work. In some cases, the research topic may be assigned by someone else rather than chosen by the researcher, but even then, from then on the main responsibility is the researcher's. So it is important to take advantage of that controlling interest and to use it wisely and well. The researcher gains some unique knowledge in the process of research, and should make sure readers understand it and appreciate its value. In the 'silent conversation' with readers which takes place through the text, we should try to present ourselves as we would wish to in a real face-to-face conversation, honestly and without either overselling or underrating ourselves. If the research has captured our enthusiasm – and it's a sad business if it hasn't done so at least at some point – then we should try to transmit that to our readers. This is not just a matter of presenting oneself in the best light to the examiners, though it is indeed important that they should form a proper estimation of the researcher as a person; more significantly, it is a unique opportunity for self-realization, which can lay the foundation for further development towards taking control of one's life and work.

And readers may be interested to know that one of things tutors and supervisors sometimes complain about is students' passivity and lack of personal identification with their research, manifesting itself in timidity, unwillingness to take initiatives, and failing to find a personal voice. *It's yours, so make the most of the chance.*

| **Example 2**
| The same project as in Example 1

Answers to the questions about the researcher's own agenda (from the checklist of Chapter 6, page 95)

7 What do I want to get out of this for myself?
8 What do I most want my readers to understand?
9 What do I want them to think and feel as a result of reading?
10 How do I want them to think of me?

What I want to get for myself from this research, besides the qualification, is:

• A full understanding of all the factors in this area, and how they interact
• The opportunity of doing something I really enjoy – going into organizations and getting people to talk to me about their work, especially the chance of doing some action research, for which I have not previously had an opportunity.

What I most want my readers to *understand* is the importance of this aspect of what organizations do; I want to share with them whatever I learn from the process of research – especially anything that indicates there are ways of doing these things that can actually help organizations to succeed better in their aims. I want them to *think* that it makes good sense, that the arguments are well sustained and supported by facts, and the conclusions legitimately drawn from the findings; and I want readers who are actually concerned with the management of information products in organizations to *feel* that any approach I advocate is worth trying. I want them to think of *me* as a reliable guide to a territory that has not been much explored by most organizations.

To make clear the key factors in the creation and presentation of information products, and how they interact, I need to show that what are usually thought of as separate activities are actually a *process* – using pictures as well as words. Because some links and interconnections are not likely to have been much considered, I shall need to make them particularly clear and build my arguments with care. In the case studies, I shall need to emphasize the individual culture of the organizations concerned, drawing on actual examples from the cases to support specific findings, and using quotations from people interviewed.

I need to make it clear to academic readers that case study organizations find this an important topic and welcome the opportunity of having it looked at – it was something I didn't wholly expect myself. I also need to show that there is shared territory between information science on the one hand and information products and presentation on the other – because some may be unaware of this (I can quote in this connection from articles I have written on the subject).

For readers in businesses and organizations, it will help establish a basis for acceptance if I can show the relationship between this aspect of their activities and initiatives that are currently popular among managers, such as business process engineering or process innovation. It will also help acceptance of what I have to say if I emphasize the methodologies which are now available for assigning reliable costs and values to information products and presentation. (I hope that this paragraph doesn't sound cynical and opportunist; if one is addressing an audience from a different professional background from one's own, it is a necessary courtesy, as well as good business, to express what one has to say in terms that are likely to be familiar to them – it helps them to accept new information and to transform it into usable knowledge more readily!)

● END OF EXAMPLE 2

The research itself

In Chapter 4, I suggested pausing at intervals to look back over the road we have travelled, to update the research map in the light of the results, and to identify new questions and new directions to investigate (see pages 63–64). This process can also yield useful ideas about what form the final product might take – ideas about structure, sequence, content and emphasis, and appropriate forms of verbal and visual presentation to match the nature of the content and the ways in which readers will want to make use of it. Because it is a reiterated process, answers will evolve and develop with each iteration, and, correspondingly, ideas about the final form of the product will become richer and more detailed.

> **Example 3**
> **The same project as in Examples 1 and 2**

Answers to the questions about the research itself (from the checklist of Chapter 6, page 96)

23 What is the purpose of the research?
24 Has it changed in the course of the research? Why?
25 How is it being carried out?
26 What are the key findings so far?
27 How do I evaluate the work done so far?
28 What are the most important things that I want readers to understand?
29 How might the research be used? What useful contribution could it make? How might it be followed up?

The purpose (as defined in Chapter 2, see page 28) so far remains unchanged. The methodology is a combination of case studies, desk research, personal communication with other practitioners in this field, and action research. So far the emphasis has been on making case studies and contacts with other practitioners.

The key findings so far from the case studies:
- Information products and presentation are not often linked with corporate strategies.
- Relevant professional skills are often not available within the organizations, and in some cases the necessity of providing for them is not appreciated.

- There is hardly any systematic pre-publication testing or post-publication evaluation.
- So far I have come across no attempts to establish the costs to organizations of inappropriate information products; but there is a strong feeling in some of the organizations that this is an area to which they ought to devote more attention.

My own evaluation so far: it seems that the research topic is a valid one, and that this is a good time to look at it because of changes in organizations and in the technologies available. There seems to be potential for linking information products with information resources as something that can be managed to support the achievement of key organizational strategies. The case study format seems to be working pretty well.

So far, the most important things I want readers to understand are:

- Information products and presentation aren't an isolated activity; they need to be integrated into the whole process of what organizations do with information to achieve their ends.
- Professional skills need to be provided for one way or another, either by employing appropriately qualified specialists in-house, or by buying in from outside
- Monitoring and evaluation of the processes of creating information products are essential.

As to the use that might be made of the research:

- Academic institutions might develop modules on information products and presentation in information management/ information science courses.
- For businesses it could make an introduction to ideas about integrated management of this aspect of their activities.
- The follow-up might include development and marketing of a product to help people with responsibility for information products in organizations. A book and/or an information pack?

These answers have useful implications for decisions on structure, sequence, content and emphasis, and appropriate forms of presentation.

STRUCTURE

This should fit the traditional thesis structure of 'Why it was done, how it was done, results of doing it, interpretation of the results and conclusions from them' – with modifications resulting from the way in which the research is being done. The case studies need careful treatment. They can be based on the reports to managements, which will be labour-saving. Probably they should be treated as a separate section, so that readers can

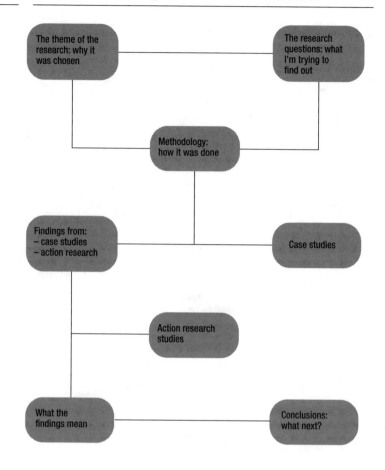

Figure 7.3a First visualization of a possible thesis structure. The main parts of the structure, put down without much attempt at sequence, but with the connections between them identified.

get the full flavour and see examples of products – that may well mean a separately bound volume for the case studies and examples; it should fit into A4 format as most examples are A4 or A5. In the main body of text, then, I can present the principal findings from the case studies – probably under the headings used in the interviews, which themselves go back to the research questions. As to the action research which I plan to do, that will probably need similar treatment, though it's difficult to be sure until I've set it up.

Figure 7.3a is a first visualization of the possible structure; it helps me to think in some more detail about sequence and division into chapters.

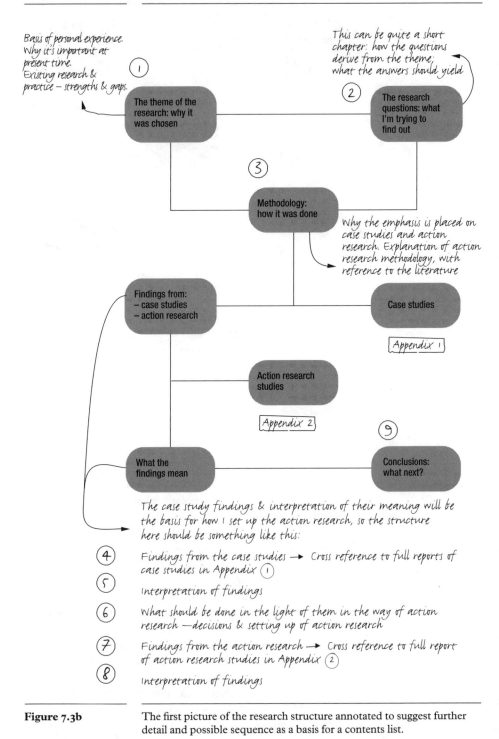

Basis of personal experience.
Why it's important at
present time.
Existing research &
practice – strengths & gaps.

① The theme of the research: why it was chosen

② The research questions: what I'm trying to find out

This can be quite a short chapter: how the questions derive from the theme; what the answers should yield

③ Methodology: how it was done

Why the emphasis is placed on case studies and action research. Explanation of action research methodology, with reference to the literature

Findings from:
– case studies
– action research

Case studies

Appendix 1

Action research studies

Appendix 2

⑨ Conclusions: what next?

What the findings mean

The case study findings & interpretation of their meaning will be the basis for how I set up the action research, so the structure here should be something like this:

④ Findings from the case studies → Cross reference to full reports of case studies in Appendix ①

⑤ Interpretation of findings

⑥ What should be done in the light of them in the way of action research —decisions & setting up of action research

⑦ Findings from the action research → Cross reference to full report of action research studies in Appendix ②

⑧ Interpretation of findings

Figure 7.3b   The first picture of the research structure annotated to suggest further detail and possible sequence as a basis for a contents list.

SEQUENCE

Figure 7.3b is a first 'contents list', based on the visualization of Figure 7.3a. It's often a help in establishing a conventional hierarchical sequence if one starts with a less formal picture which captures the key elements without trying to make decisions about how they should be broken down or what order they should be taken in.

1 Why this subject?
   The basis of personal experience, and the need for a formal study of the area
   Why it's important at the present time
   Previous work in the area; what existing research and practice suggest
2 The research questions
3 Methodology and why
   How the case studies and the action research were set up
4 Findings from the case studies (cross-reference to detailed case study reports)
5 What the findings mean
6 Decisions about action research in the light of the case study findings
7 What happened in the action research
8 Interpretation of what happened in the action research
9 Final conclusions – what next?

Appendices
   Case study reports
   Action research report
   Outline product developed during action research

CONTENT AND EMPHASIS

The main content is indicated in the paragraphs above about structure and sequence. So far as things to emphasize are concerned:

• The review of relevant research and practice should emphasize the well-established lessons, and the gaps where little or no work has been done.
• The findings from actual organizations are the most important content, and need to be very clearly presented and strongly supported.
• Proposals for addressing the problems, and the results of trying them out, are also of key importance. Here the emphasis needs to be on the foundation for proposals and on what

actually happened. This is the high-risk area; I have to be
prepared for the unexpected and ready to highlight it and the
causes.

APPROPRIATE FORMS OF PRESENTATION
Quite a lot of narrative text, with quotations from sources.
Summaries and lists for presenting key findings. Diagrams for
organizational structures, information flows and processes
involved in creating information products. A lot of cross-
references. Heading hierarchy won't need to be too deep.
Typographic distinction between main text and case studies/
action research?

      ● END OF EXAMPLE 3

A summary of the decisions you should be able to get from this round of questions and answers

ANSWERS ABOUT USERS
- Where you are likely to know more than they do: don't take
  knowledge on their part for granted, try to find a starting point
  where they do have knowledge, and then lead them carefully
  on, step by step, without expecting them to make jumps. Define any unfamiliar terms which you have to use the *first* time
  you introduce them.

- Where they have expert knowledge: show that you appreciate
  it. Don't give them elementary explanations of concepts or
  summaries of books that are well known to them – try to show
  your knowledge more subtly.

- Try to keep as far as possible to forms of presentation that are
  familiar to them, but don't force your material into a form
  that's not appropriate for it. If you decide the product needs to
  be presented in a form that is very different from what they're
  used to, prepare the ground beforehand with your tutors, and
  explain the reasons for the departure from tradition very clearly in the introduction to the product itself.

ANSWERS ABOUT YOUR OWN AGENDA
Take them into account in making decisions about style of presentation. How do you establish yourself as a real person without
putting yourself too much in the foreground at the expense of the
research itself? Places where you can legitimately take centre
stage are: the introduction or preface, where the author plays a

role like that of the host welcoming guests to his/her own house and doing the honours; wherever you are writing about work that involved personal interaction between you and others in the interests of the research, such as interviews, experiments, testing; evaluation of what has come out of the research; and, of course, in any supporting document you have to submit like an assessment contract or personal evaluation of your research.

ANSWERS ABOUT THE RESEARCH

- If the purpose, hypothesis, questions, or emphasis of the research have undergone major change, you need to make that very clear at the outset. It will help readers to follow your mental path, and avoid them asking irrelevant questions or coming to erroneous conclusions.

- Similarly with methodology – if you've found it necessary to modify the methods you originally proposed, explain why; justify your final choice so that it can be understood clearly, even if the readers themselves might not have made the same choice. (See Chapter 4, pages 63 and 65, on using your documentation on methodology as the basis for your chapter on how the research was done.)

- The key findings so far – especially the unexpected ones – will suggest ideas for the structure for presenting your findings, and where to place emphasis.

- The things you most want readers to understand are likely to be those where you yourself have gained most understanding, and again they will suggest ideas about structure and emphasis, particularly in the interpretation of findings and the conclusions you draw.

- All this should help to establish first ideas for sequence: how the end product might be divided up into chapters or sections, and what links will be needed to help your readers to move easily among your ideas. As Figure 7.4 on page 112 shows, one needs 'vertical' links between one chapter and the next, and 'horizontal' ones between what is said on a topic in one place and other relevant passages elsewhere.

- It should also help the decisions on what to put in, what to omit, what to emphasize; and how to deal with detailed data – whether certain information should go into an appendix for instance.

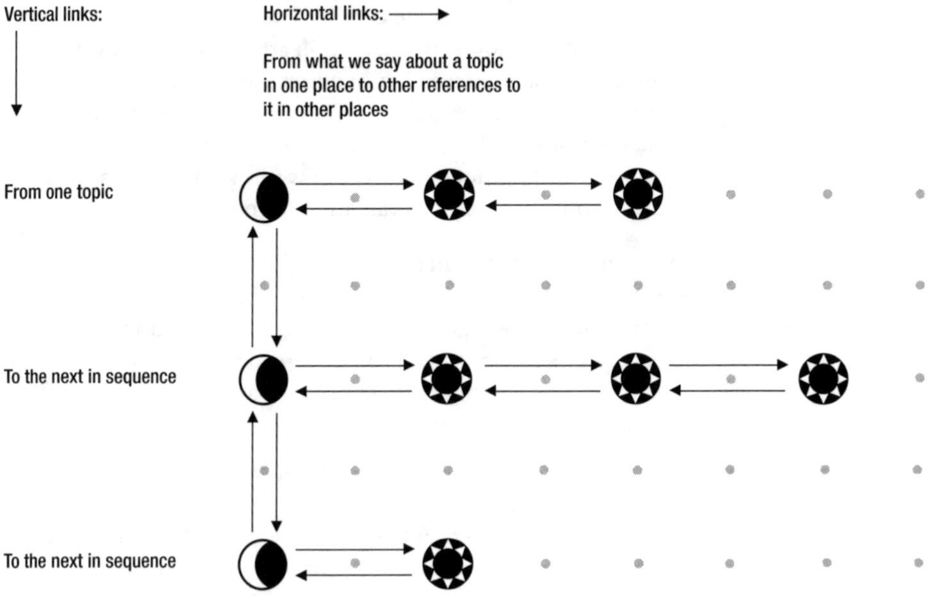

Vertical links:

Horizontal links: ⟶

From what we say about a topic in one place to other references to it in other places

From one topic

To the next in sequence

To the next in sequence

Figure 7.4   'Vertical' and 'horizontal' links. Note that the links go both ways; we may need to refer both forwards and backwards.

- The nature of the content, eg how much numerical data, how much presentation of interrelationships between findings, will suggest first decisions on appropriate forms of presentation and the kinds of information elements you will need – will it be appropriate to use tables, lists, diagrams, as well as prose narrative? (There is more about this in Chapters 8 and 9.)

- Ideas about the utility of the research, and how you yourself might follow it up, are handy for the final chapter; it's always a good idea to leave the door ajar at the end, with a pointer to what might follow.

What next?

In Chapter 8 we look at what these decisions imply for choosing ways of presenting our research.

8 | Extending our repertoire for presenting information

'and what is the use of a book,' thought Alice, 'without pictures or conversations?'

(LEWIS CARROLL, *Alice's Adventures in Wonderland*, 1865,
Chapter 1)

I start this chapter by asking readers a question that I usually put to any group of people with whom I am talking about writing:

> When you find a text – a book, an article, a report, for instance – that you know is likely to contain something that will be useful to you, what features make it difficult for you to get at the useful information?

The 'top turn-offs' are given later in the chapter (see page 130); for the moment, it is enough to say that most people's pet hate is acres of unrelieved prose. I find this a strange contrast; we dislike it when we have to fight our way through it, yet prose composition is the main thing we have to do with our written language at school and in higher education. Most of us get little opportunity of learning about the rich range of alternatives to prose for conveying information, and how to make good use of them. So this chapter is about some of the most useful alternative ways of presenting information, and how to make a choice of them to match:

- The nature of the information itself
- The people who will use it
- The ways in which they will want to use it.

It deals, among other things, with presenting information in words (in various ways besides just continuous prose), in numbers (in various kinds of table and diagram), and in graphic form. It also looks at how we can provide signposts to help readers through the text, and at establishing standards for the presentation of various 'information elements'.

Figure 8.1 shows how the three factors of the nature of the information, the people who will want to use it, and the ways in

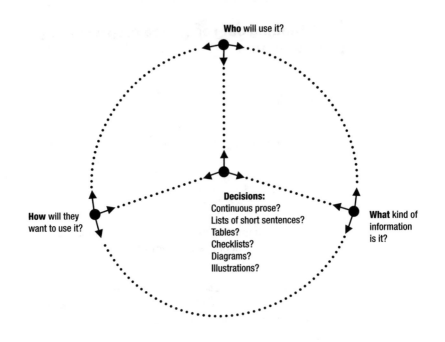

Figure 8.1   The nature of information, the users, and the ways in which they will
want to use it, can interact to shape decisions about presentation.

which they will want to use it – what, who and how – can interact
to shape our decisions about the ways in which we present information.

Promoting the conversation with readers

In the 'conversation' with readers which we undertake in present-
ing the information products of research, we need to do a variety
of things. As we saw in the last chapter, they are likely to include:
- Showing the structure of the product
- Helping readers to find their way around the structure by
  means of 'signposts' of various kinds
- Directing attention to key points
- Telling readers what they are about to encounter, and sum-
  marizing what they have just been told ('previews and reviews')
- Telling the 'story' of the research
- Defining terms
- Presenting relevant material from the sources we have used
- Explaining the methods used in the research

- Presenting sequences and flows of events
- Distinguishing between parts of text which perform different functions
- Presenting the results of research – both qualitative and quantitative.

Options for presentation

The examples in Chapter 7 indicated the options for some of these things that seemed appropriate for a specific piece of research. This section deals with each item of the list above, and suggests some appropriate ways of presentation that take into account the 'what, who and how'.

SHOWING THE STRUCTURE OF THE PRODUCT

In Chapter 7 (see pages 106 to 108) we showed the development of an outline contents list for a dissertation. Such a list gives both sequence and basic hierarchy. Within each chapter or section, further structural pointers in the way of headings of various levels will be needed in the final product. Heading hierarchies should not be allowed to become too deep! If in planning the sub-divisions of a chapter you find that the number of levels of heading exceeds four, it is wise to ask whether you are trying to get too much into the chapter, and whether it would benefit by being split into two chapters. Human memory has difficulty in remembering where it is when there are too many levels of hierarchy, and too many visual distinctions between them to recall, and so the benefits of showing different levels turn into hindrances. (See Chapter 9 for visual ways of distinguishing levels of heading, and Chapter 10 for more about final decisions about sub-divisions and what goes into them.)

Figure 8.2a on page 116 shows the development of sub-headings for a chapter of a research report (the method is similar to that shown for developing a structure for presenting a complete report in Figure 7.3b), and Figure 8.2b on page 117 shows the use of distinguishing letters which is the customary way of showing the different levels of the hierarchy of sub-headings.

HELPING READERS TO FIND THEIR WAY AROUND THE STRUCTURE BY MEANS OF 'SIGNPOSTS' OF VARIOUS KINDS

Readers of research products are likely to want to read in various ways besides sequentially; they may well want to enter the text at various points to look at something specific, to follow particular

Project title:
*Factors influencing the
application of economic
thresholds for insect
pest control in field crops
by farmers in East Anglia*

Chapter title:
*How East Anglian farmers
make decisions about
pesticide application*

A picture of the topics to
be covered in the chapter,
as a basis for developing a
hierarchy of sub-headings

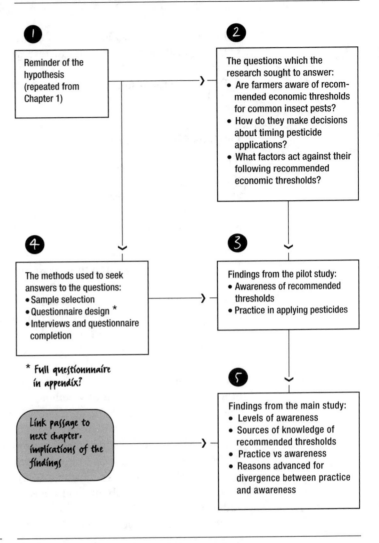

Figure 8.2a   Developing a chapter structure for a research report.

themes which appear at various points, and to refer back and forward. Elements that assist this kind of movement include indexes
to help in entering the text at specific points, cross-references for
horizontal movement between chapters, and various forms of
navigation aid for particular groups of readers who approach the
text with different purposes. (See Chapter 9 for visual treatment
of these elements).

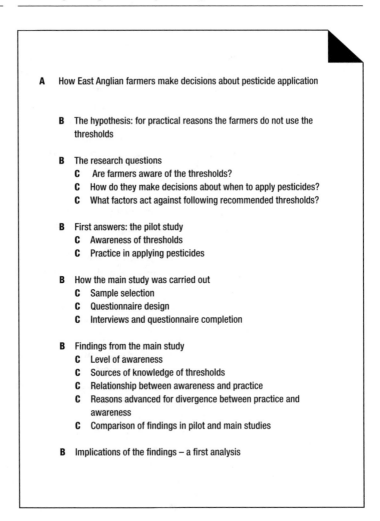

A   How East Anglian farmers make decisions about pesticide application

B   The hypothesis: for practical reasons the farmers do not use the thresholds

B   The research questions
   C   Are farmers aware of the thresholds?
   C   How do they make decisions about when to apply pesticides?
   C   What factors act against following recommended thresholds?

B   First answers: the pilot study
   C   Awareness of thresholds
   C   Practice in applying pesticides

B   How the main study was carried out
   C   Sample selection
   C   Questionnaire design
   C   Interviews and questionnaire completion

B   Findings from the main study
   C   Level of awareness
   C   Sources of knowledge of thresholds
   C   Relationship between awareness and practice
   C   Reasons advanced for divergence between practice and awareness
   C   Comparison of findings in pilot and main studies

B   Implications of the findings – a first analysis

Figure 8.2b   A heading hierarchy derived from the chapter structure shown in Figure 8.2a

DIRECTING READERS' ATTENTION TO KEY POINTS
One of the things readers most dislike is pages of undifferentiated text, with no visible cues as to its content or structure. In every chapter or section of a research product there are likely to be key points that the reader needs to understand in order to stay with the author. They occur typically at the end of chapters, but also at various stages in narrative or argument and they should not be

given an obscure burial in prose paragraphs. The lead up to them may well be in prose, but if there are distinct observations to be made or conclusions to be drawn, they should be shown as distinct. The usual options are numbered or bulleted lists for a series of points, or displayed paragraphs for single key points (see Chapter 9 for ways of visual presentation of lists.)

If there is a key distinction to be made within an individual sentence – to make a particular word stand out, or to show a contrast, *italic* or **bold** are the usual options (see Chapter 9 for more examples).

TELLING READERS WHAT THEY ARE ABOUT TO ENCOUNTER, AND SUMMARIZING WHAT THEY HAVE JUST BEEN TOLD ('PREVIEWS AND REVIEWS')

Researchers, by the time they come to write about their research, are usually so familiar with and absorbed in their subject that they can move about it in their minds as easily as we move through the streets of a familiar town. It is hard to realize that readers – even those who have expert knowledge in the general area of the research – don't share that familiarity, and that they can easily get out of breath and lose the thread of the argument as they are hauled from idea to idea. They need pausing places where they can look back over the route so far, and survey what lies immediately ahead. We can provide them by means of recapitulations of the key points made in the chapter they have just read, and outlines of what the current chapter will deal with. This is another place where the displayed list can be useful – especially for recapitulating; for previewing, either an introductory sentence or paragraph, or a displayed list can do the job.

TELLING THE 'STORY' OF THE RESEARCH

Most research products follow an essentially chronological path; they start from the beginning and tell the reader what happened in the course of the research, and so they involve a good deal of narrative. They also, by the very nature of research, require a lot of development of arguments – why a particular question was chosen for investigation, why a specific method was selected, the reasoning that supports the interpretation advanced for findings. It is here that prose comes into its own – it's hard to beat for telling a story, making an argument, and developing a chain of ideas (though even for these purposes it can profitably be supported by other non-prose forms of communication, such as flowcharts for showing a course of events, displayed lists for key conclusions, and diagrams to represent relationships between ideas).

In presenting ideas and topics that may be new to readers it's important to take them at a gentle pace which involves none of the jumps and short-cuts that we can cope with when we are dealing with the familiar. So we need to start from ideas familiar to them, and show how they relate to the new ideas, to introduce new ones a step at a time, to make clear links between one idea and the next, and to provide stopping places of the kind described above.

DEFINING TERMS

Not long ago I was talking with someone planning to start on an MEd course. He was reading a book on educational testing, and finding it heavy going because it contained so many new terms whose meaning he had to absorb. They were getting in the way of actually reading the book, because the author had not given sufficient attention to defining them and to helping readers to form a clear idea of what they meant. So he was forced to write his own definitions and try to learn the meaning before going on with reading. He also complained that there were hardly any examples to make the definitions clear in practical terms. If you look at page 130 you will see that failure to explain unfamiliar terms adequately as soon as they appear is high on most people's list of turn-offs – and rightly so, because it is a check to understanding that halts us in our tracks and makes the time we devote to reading less productive than it ought to be.

So, identify for yourself the terms that are likely to need defining for some if not all of your readers (ask friends and colleagues to check your text for others when you start writing), and decide on how you will treat them.

Unacceptable ways of handling definitions
- A glossary at the back of the dissertation is *not* acceptable as the sole means of defining terms. Readers need on-the-spot explanation as soon as they find an unfamiliar term. If they have to move from the page they are reading and find the term in an alphabetical list, they will have lost the thread of what they are reading by the time they have done so.
- For the same reason, even a definition in a footnote on the same page can lead to a break in concentration.

Better ways
- Displayed definitions immediately after new terms
- Marginal definitions alongside them

- In-text definitions that unobtrusively make the meaning explicit (useful for situations where some readers will know perfectly well and others won't, and you don't want to insult those who know).

For example:

> We can look at a book or a report as being made up of *information elements* – each of which has its own function in showing the structure of the text (as headings do), or pointing the way through it to specific information (contents lists, indexes, and cross-references, for example), or conveying a particular kind of information (as tables and diagrams do for numerical information).

PRESENTING RELEVANT MATERIAL FROM THE SOURCES WE HAVE USED

This essential element of research products is often handled in such an uninspired way that the contribution it could make loses most of its value. Chapter 10 (pages 174–176) deals with the process of writing about this kind of material; here we look at some of the options for presenting it.

However we decide to solve the problem of presenting material from sources, there are two essentials that must be treated consistently: quotations from the sources and references to them – in the text itself and in lists of the sources cited.

Quotations should not be too lengthy – if for no other reason than copyright (although British copyright law, unlike that of the USA, does not set actual limits on the number of words you may quote without applying for permission to reproduce them, it is safer to limit quotations to no more than a sentence or two). Apart from that, short, apposite quotations are more effective – they show the author is in command of his/her sources rather than in thrall to them.

When you quote phrases rather than whole sentences, incorporate them in your own sentence. Longer quotations, of whole sentences, are better displayed, so that they can be seen as separate from the text.

So far as references are concerned, the 'Harvard' system, as used in this book, is the easiest one to handle, because it doesn't involve keeping numbered references in order (very difficult when you make changes in the sequence of the text).

Lists of key points are a useful way of showing the main conclusions from a range of sources on a specific topic. Figure 8.3 shows an example.

The literature is well epitomised by Bowden and Ricketts (1992), and by such studies as those of Fransman (1992) and Newby (1993). Another useful summary of the literature on the subject, with special reference to critical innovation factors at various stages of innovation, is given by Johannessen and Olaisen (1993).

Among the points relevant to the value of information are these:

- R&D investment is a necessary but not a sufficient condition for successful innovation. Successful innovative firms keep a close eye on the market, and on demographic and social change; and they spend a lot of time listening to their customers.

- R&D is a 'capital stock of knowledge which can be built up over time but which depreciates' (Bowden & Ricketts, 1992, pp3–31) – so it needs feeding and maintaining by constant new inputs of information. And the maintenance depends on 'managerial and organisational skills to apply' the inputs of information (Newby, 1993)

- A well educated and skilled labour force helps innovation because 'it makes it easier to introduce new technology successfully and to develop techniques by drawing upon workers' informal knowledge and experience' (Bowden and Ricketts, 1992, p44) and it increases the pool from which new ideas come

(1)

Figure 8.3   Lists of key points to show the main conclusions from a range of sources on a specific topic: an extract from a summary of the literature on what makes for success in innovation

Table 1.2 Factors inhibiting information technology transfer *

General factors	Conditions in developing countries
1 Economic	Labour-intensive society
	Low availability of capital
	Inability to absorb recurring costs
	Expense of international activities
	Lack of internal competition
2 Manpower	Lack of available trained personnel
	Low prestige of information professionals
	Difficulty in recruiting specialists
	Lack of continuing education
	Inexperience of working in teams

Adapted from Eres, 1981, pp. 97–102 *

Figure 8.4   Part of a table summarizing the key information from a particular source. (Reproduced from a doctoral thesis by Simon Bell).

Tabulated presentation of text is another useful method of briefly summarizing key features from important sources, as shown in Figure 8.4.

If certain sources have been important in your choice of methodology, 'compare and contrast tables' can be useful for differentiating between approaches, as shown in Figure 8.5.

EXPLAINING THE METHODS USED IN THE RESEARCH
Chapter 4 (see page 63) recommended recording the formats you develop for applying methods, such as questionnaires, interview schedules, and protocols for carrying out experiments. Actual examples of them, with minimal connecting text, are the best way of demonstrating your methods.

PRESENTING SEQUENCES OF EVENTS, RELATIONSHIPS AND STRUCTURES OF IDEAS
If you need to tell readers about a sequence of events and the people involved in it, a flowchart is useful for giving a quick and clear picture.

For showing organizational structures and the way information flows in them, useful options are diagrams which incorporate flowchart elements (see Figure 8.6 on page 124) and 'rich pictures' (see Figure 8.7 on page 125).

Table 7.6 Multiview methodology: a comparison before and after the third piece of field work.

Stage and link	Multiview after field work 1	Multiview after field work 2	Multiview after field work 3
Pre-analysis and analysis preparation.	Self-analysis of the analyst and preparatory tools specifically related to interview techniques	Indications of the need to develop pre-project analysis of recipient and donor.	Further evidence for the need for pre-project analysis of all actors. Information from stage 1.
Stage 1 the human activity system	As the original plus standardized glossary of diagram tools for rich picture, multiple use of root definitions to cross check results, conceptual models.	As in the first field work but some freedom given to recipients to adapt the use of tools.	Valuable insights gained from the use of the soft tools. Specifically relating to the different perceptions of the project focus by the various actors.

Figure 8.5   Part of a table to show how methodology was progressively modified in the course of field work for a research project. (Reproduced from a doctoral thesis by Simon Bell).

Diagrams are also a very useful way of helping readers to see the interrelations of ideas; Figure 8.8, on page 126, shows how various forms of mental activity can work together to resolve problems and find creative solutions.

All these diagrammatic forms have the advantage that they can show both sequence and simultaneity – they are not tied to the linearity of prose description, and the eye and mind can move about them freely in 'reading the content'. The power of graphic means of conveying information is indeed not sufficiently regarded or understood, even by those who habitually use them. The richness and variety available are eloquently described and displayed in Edward R Tufte's beautiful book on 'envisioning' information (1990: 9):

> To envision information – and what bright and splendid visions can result – is to work at the intersection of image, word, number, art. The instruments are those of writing and typography, of managing large data sets and statistical analysis, of line and layout and color. And the standards of quality are those derived from visual principles that tell us how to put the right mark in the right place.

Those who are particularly interested in presenting quantitative information by graphic means will find Tufte's other book on the subject (1983) a fascinating source of reference, with a vast

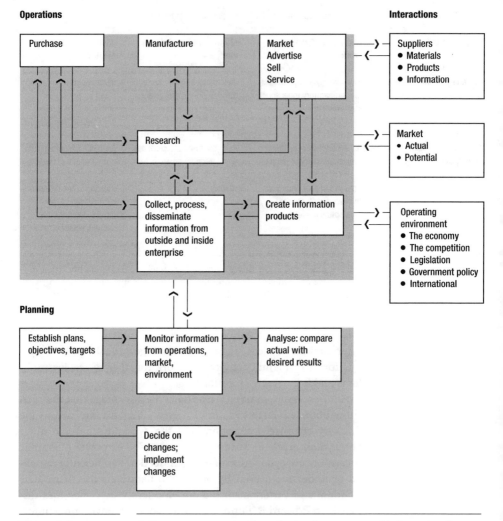

Figure 8.6   A diagram representing organizational structure and information flow.
From: Orna, E. *Practical information policies.* Gower, Aldershot, 1990.

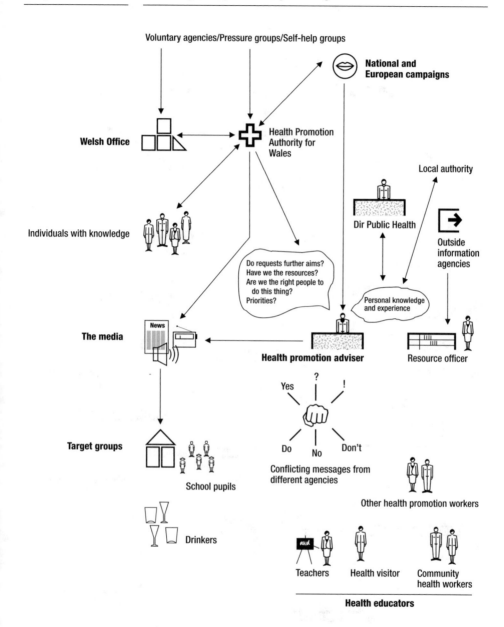

Figure 8.7   A 'rich picture' of an organization, showing the context of its work and the major participating groups. Based on *International Journal of Information Management,* 12, Hepworth, J.B. *et al,* The enhancement of information systems through user involvement in system design, 120–129 (1992), with kind permission from Butterworth-Heinemann journals, Elsevier Science Limited, The Boulevard, Langford Lane, Kidlington OX5 1GB, UK.

[125]

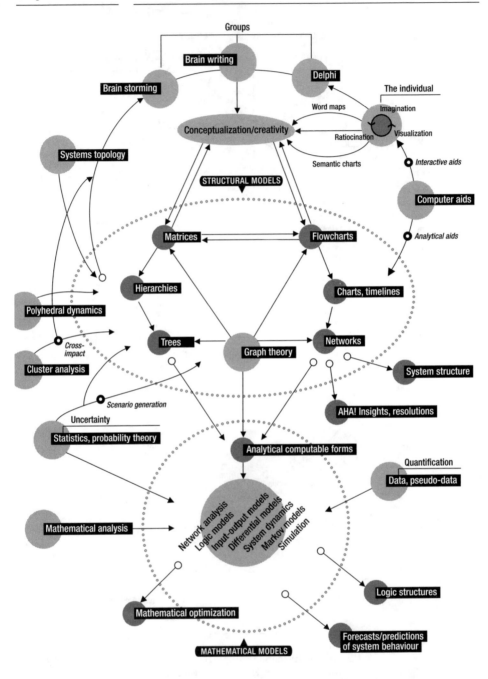

Figure 8.8   A diagram showing the interaction of different ways of creating mental models. From M'Pherson, P. K. (1985) *Systems engineering training programmes.* MacPherson Systems Limited, 1985.

variety of examples, good and bad. (The power of diagrammatic presentation is well known to, but unfortunately often misused by, large companies; a study (Beattie and Jones, 1994: 225) of the annual reports of over 200 leading businesses in the UK showed evidence of '…systematic selectivity, measurement distortion and presentational enhancement … we found that companies were three times more likely to include graphs in their annual report which exaggerated, rather than understated, a rising trend.')

DISTINGUISHING BETWEEN PARTS OF TEXT WHICH PERFORM DIFFERENT FUNCTIONS

You may want to comment on or amplify what is in the main text, or to show text and a numerical or visual interpretation of it. If readers are to get the benefit of this, eye and mind need to be able to move easily between the related parts, and that means they should be in the same plane and visually distinct. If one follows end-on from the other, it is hard for the reader to make sense of the comparison. Commentary can run alongside main text or appear in marginal annotations; pages can be divided horizontally or vertically between text and graphics, or between main text and detailed material. (A caution, though, relating to running commentary alongside text – if it is pursued through several pages, so that readers effectively have to follow two strands simultaneously, it can demand too much of eye and brain, so it should be used with discretion.)

PRESENTING THE RESULTS – QUANTITATIVE AND QUALITATIVE TABLES

In most research there are points at which we need to allow readers to compare items of information and inspect the conclusions we draw from them. This is particularly so if the research has involved tests, experiments, or surveys, but it can also be necessary in less formal investigations, like case studies, which yield little that can be counted but still permit of putting the findings into categories and making statements about the categories.

If we want readers to be able to do that, then we need a systematic arrangement of the items that we wish readers to compare, inspect, etc. Tables are a well-established and potentially very efficient way of putting information into non-linear form to help people to think about it. They can be entirely numeric, entirely verbal, or mixed.

Guidelines from one study of the factors that make for ease or difficulty in using tables to find information (Wright and Fox, 1970) include the following points:

- Full and direct presentation of the information users will need (don't ask them to draw inferences or to combine information from different parts of the table).
- Vertical arrangement of items within the table.
- Grouping items within columns by the use of spacing – blocks of about five items give good results.
- Omit redundant abbreviations within the body of the table – put the appropriate unit signs at the head of the column.
- Use minimal space between related pairs of items in adjacent columns – that is, close proximity between the information looked up and that read off.
- Left to right arrangement of columns so that information is read off to the right of the item looked up.

Laslett (1979) gives some useful advice on two common kinds of statistical table:

1 Reference tables, which can be used as a source of data for various purposes
2 Special-purpose tables, which are used to convey a particular message and highlight specific points, usually in conjunction with text.

Reference tables should make no attempt to draw the reader's eye to significant relationships; the main essential is clarity and consistency so that readers can easily use them for extracting whatever data they need.

Special-purpose tables should not seek to convey too much information in any one table; it is often better to break down related data into a series of tables so that different features can be examined one at a time. There is a lower limit, too; in practice, the smallest amount of information worth putting in a table consists of two rows and two columns. The figures in special-purpose tables should be given to a degree of accuracy that makes clear the message that the writer is trying to convey; often comparisons and contrasts are made more evident by expressing figures in thousands or hundreds, rather than to two decimal places. Ranking data from highest to lowest for a particular feature can also help to emphasize a point. Comparing columns is easier than comparing rows.

When tables are used within text, there should always be a clear reference to each in the text. Table titles should always state clearly the subject of the table, the nature of the data, and the factors by which the data are analysed. The source of numerical data in tables should always be indicated.

Don't try to put numerical information in prose. This extract from an article about a survey of students' computer use should help to show why it's not a good idea.

> Our survey took the form of a questionnaire from which we got a response of 79%. From this amount 15.8% declared they did not use the computer at all and 63.2% did. The figure of 63.2% can be further broken down in that 26.3% of the users were female and 36.9% were male. Of the 63.2% who did use the computer in some form, none had all their work stored on a computer file. 10.5% had 90% of their work on file and 5.26% had 10% of their work stored. A figure of 15.8% had 50% of their work stored, with the same figure applying to those having 5% or less stored. 5.28% had 70% and 25% stored respectively, with those who had between 10% – 20% stored amounting to a similar figure of 5.28%.

The information elements you need

Use the checklist below to identify the the information elements that are likely to be useful for your own combination of readers, content, and ways of use, and for which you will need to establish standards. For some elements, like references, there are well-established standards, which form part of a 'house style' – the set of conventions which organizations or individuals apply in all their information products. For others, such as tables and headings, design decisions will be needed to arrive at standards which allow comfortable integration of all the elements involved – and you will find help for this in Chapter 9 (see the Appendix to the chapter for examples of design solutions).

A checklist of information elements

TYPE OF DATA	TICK IF PRESENT	SEE PAGE
1 HEADINGS		
'A' headings:		155
'B' level		155
'C' level		155
'D' level		155
2 SIGNPOSTS:		
Index		160
Cross-references		158
Displayed key paragraphs		157
Emphasis within sentences		157

Checklist /continued	TYPE OF DATA	TICK IF PRESENT	SEE PAGE
	Previews		161
	Recapitulations		161
	3 NARRATIVE:		
	Sentences		
	Paragraphs		156
	4 Definitions		160
	5 Questionnaires		
	6 Flow diagrams		159
	7 Diagrams		
	8 Illustrations		
	9 TABLES:		
	Numeric with text		158
	Text only		
	10 Lists		157
	11 Detailed text to supplement main text		
	12 Text commentary on graphics and/or tables		

Top turn-offs

You may have wondered what has happened to the list of turn-offs that I promised at the start of this chapter. Here it is; the things that people usually rank first are:

- Unexplained unfamiliar words
- Lots of 'grey' text with no headings
- Complicated sentences in which the reader gets lost
- Illustrations and tables remote from the relevant text
- Unclear links between ideas.

And here is an expanded guide to ways in which writers can lose readers; it comes from a module on *Writing to Inform* in a course on desktop publishing design for non-designers (Stevens):

- Don't tell them the things they need to know in order to understand what comes next.
- Use lots of technical words without explaining them; or if you do explain them, don't do it the first time you use them – that should make sure the readers lose the thread while wondering what they mean.
- Work hard at writing long-winded sentences that take a long time to grasp.
- Show off your membership of the in-group by using jargon words.
- Give them pages and pages of solid text with no headings.

- Make them jump from one topic to the next; the exercise is good for them, and with luck you'll throw them off.
- Make them run around for the information they need for understanding, instead of putting it all together in the same place; that should help to make sure they'll lose their grasp of the argument, if you haven't made it obscure enough already.
- Never put diagrams and tables on the same page as the text about them.
- Make sure that the text tells a different story from the numbers in the tables.

References

Beattie, V. and Jones, M. J. (1994) Information design and manipulation: financial graphs in corporate annual reports, *Information Design Journal* 7 (3): 211–226.

Bell, S. (1994) *Towards an eclectic approach to information systems development: lessons from the application of Multiview in two developing countries.* PhD thesis. Norwich: University of East Anglia.

Hepworth, J. B.(1992) *et al* The enhancement of information systems through user involvement in system design, *International Journal of Information Management* 12: 120–129

Laslett, R. E. (1979) Presenting information in tables and diagrams, in E. Orna, and R. E. Laslett *Writing to Inform.* Watford: Engineering Industry Training Board Research Division.

M'Pherson, P.K. (1985) *Systems Engineering Training Programmes.* Kenninghall, Norfolk: MacPherson Systems Ltd.

Orna, E. (1990) *Practical Information Policies.* Aldershot: Gower

Stevens, G. (forthcoming) *DTP typography for non-designers.* Reading: Department of Typography and Graphic Communication, University of Reading.

Tufte, E. R. (1983) *The Visual Display of Quantitative Information.* Cheshire, Connecticut: Graphics Press.

Tufte, E. R. (1990) *Envisioning Information.* Cheshire, Connecticut: Graphics Press.

Wright, P. and Fox, K. (1970) Presenting information in tables, *Applied Ergonomics,* 1: 234–242.

9 | Design is more than cosmetic!

This chapter was jointly written with the information designer Graham Stevens; the introduction is mine, but all the really useful parts are his.

Good visual design is serious in purpose ... Each individual problem requires objective answers to three basic questions: (a) what is the purpose of the information? [to determine design needs], (b) what is the information content? [to evaluate design means] and (c) what is the information's relation to other information forms which precede or follow it? [to develop design continuity]. The concept of design as a process of objective thinking is less obvious, but the most important characteristic of the 'new graphic design'. (SUTNAR, 1961)

Introduction: the design of information

Unfortunately researchers are seldom aware that it's worth giving a clear visual structure even to early drafts and documents written for internal consumption. When MA students give me draft chapters to read, I often have to point out that the form in which they are presented makes them time-consuming to read and understand, and just about impossible to annotate. The most frequent obstacles to doing what I am supposed to do in order to help the writers are:

- Overlong lines and lack of adequate margins, producing pages which have the appearance of being too densely set, and which are certainly more difficult to read.
- Lack of inter-line spacing
- Lack of sub-headings
- Undue attachment to continuous prose, which leads to information which is really a series of points being uncomfortably embedded in knotty sentences.

If such obstacles are allowed to persist into the final version, the examiners may not formulate a complaint as precisely as that, but they are likely to have a sense of malaise and irritation which will do the candidate no good at all.

From many years of working with information designers and observing them at work, I have learned that such apparently indifferent matters as initial page size and layout, positioning of information elements, choice of typeface, treatment of headings, captions, the spacing of characters, words and lines, etc., can actually make the difference between an attractive and accessible product and one that is repellent and hard to get at.

The 'information designer' specializes in understanding the structure of the products he/she designs, entering into the writer's intentions, and finding visual ways of making intentions clear and structure apparent. As a writer, I have been fortunate enough to work closely with an information designer, and I still have not got used to the surprise and pleasure of seeing my thoughts brought to life on the page by intelligent and sympathetic design – which really becomes part of the information I am trying to present and enhances the communication.

While the knowledge and skills of information designers are long in the learning (their education takes as long as that of engineers, accountants, or historians, and the full development of their expertise takes many more years), there are some basic aspects of their understanding that non-designers can profitably make part of their equipment for presenting the products of research. This chapter looks at what happens when we read, and how choice of typeface and type size, spacing, and page organization can make the task of the reader easier or more difficult; and it suggests practical steps to making choices that are appropriate for the kind of product we are presenting.

| DEFINITION   Information design

...all the activities which go to making ideas visible, to showing their structure and the relations between them – so that others can use them and make them their own... a special case of the general human activity of designing, which consists of finding an expressive structure that allows communication between human beings. It is special because:
- *The products have a high information content, usually expressed in words, but frequently including drawings, diagrams and photographs, if these help to clarify the content.*
- *Information designers see users as an active initiating force, who consciously know they want certain information, and who want it in order to use it for purposes they themselves have defined.* ❱

(Orna and Stevens, 1991)

Information design is an integral part of communicating; it takes part in the 'conversations' that help users of information to resolve anomalies in knowledge, and permit new 'commitments' (Winograd and Flores, 1986) and actions. It is an actual part of the visible information into which knowledge is transformed and from which knowledge is reconstituted.

| DEFINITION   Typography

The typographer requires knowledge and skill in:
- *Analysing the overall document with regard to the kind of inform- ation that has to be communicated*
- *Asking appropriate questions, and then planning the individual page structure, with regard to the overall document plan, and finding an- swers to particular features of the information that have been identi- fied as necessary, such as hierarchical order of headings*
- *Choosing the most appropriate typeface, size, line length, inter-line and inter-word spacing; and taking into account the system and soft- ware being used to generate the type*
- *Ensuring that the finished document is printed on the most suitable paper, and that any print finishing is appropriate and functional.* ❱

How we read, and what it means for design

The way in which the human eye and mind behave when we read has important implications for design, with regard to reading, and the avoidance of visual ambiguity in the treatment of all the discrete typographical elements, such as headings. In reading, we scan *groups* of words, not individual words, and in scanning it is the top of letter forms that gives the clue to the word picture. The eye moves along in a series of jumps, and not in a smooth flowing action; the movement is so fast that it is impossible to have a clear vision of what is being read. Perception occurs only during 'fixa- tion pauses' which last in the adult reader for about a quarter of a second. If there is doubt about the sense, the eye moves back- wards towards the beginning of the line. At the end of a line, the eye makes a 'return sweep' towards the next line to be read (see Figure 9.1).

Decisions about typeface, type size and line length, and about the incremental units of spacing used to separate lines, words and individual characters have a strong influence on how easy it is to read and understand text.

The eye moves along the line in a series of jumps. Perception occurs only during the stops (fixation pauses) which last in the adult reader for between one fifth and one twentieth of a second

Figure 9.1	The process of reading.

LINE LENGTH

A line length (or *measure*) that accommodates between 52 and 65 characters is comfortable to read. Translated into word averages for the English language, it approximates to between eight and eleven words to a line.

It is very common to select too long a measure, particularly when using A4 paper sizes. Overlong lines make for difficulty in reading because the eye has to make more backward movements, and is liable to alight on the wrong line during its back and forth movement; this slows down reading and understanding.

If lines are very short,
on the other hand,
reading is also made
more difficult; breaking
up the sentences into
very small word groups
causes the eye to make
too many backward
movements.

Readability rule 1	In continuous text, lines should be between 52 and 65 characters for maximum ease of reading.

SPACING BETWEEN LINES

line feeds of 12 pts	The space that separates one line of type from its neighbour is
11 pts	also very important in the process of reading, for these strips of
10 pts	white space help the eye to separate one line from another. It is
solid 9.5 pts	possible to set type *solid*, that is, without any additional inter-line
8 pt	space, and where the distance from one base-line to the next is
7 pts	the same as the type size, or even with *minus* inter-line spacing.
12 pts	Setting type solid is acceptable if the type has a small x-height
12 pts	with long ascenders and descenders, and the measures used are
12 pts	relatively short. Setting type with minus interline spacing is to be
12 pts	avoided at all times, as this inevitably results in ascenders and
12 pts	descenders clashing or overlapping. This will destroy the normal

Primary heading

Secondary heading

xxxxxxxxxxxxxxxxxxxxxxxxxxxxxxxxxxxxxxxxxx
xxxxxxxxxxxxxxxxxxxxxxxxxxxxxxxxxxxxxxxxxx
xxxxxxxxxxxxxxxxxxxxxxxxxxxxxxxxxxxxxxxxxx

xxxxxxxxxxxxxxxxxxxxxxxxxxxxxxxxxxxxxxxxxx
xxxxxxxxxxxxxxxxxxxxxxxxxxxxxxxxxxxxxxxxxx
xxxxxxxxxxxxxxxxxxxxxxxxxxxxxxxxxxxxxxxxxx

Tertiary heading

xxxxxxxxxxxxxxxxxxxxxxxxxxxxxxxxxxxxxxxxxx
xxxxxxxxxxxxxxxxxxxxxxxxxxxxxxxxxxxxxxxxxx
xxxxxxxxxxxxxxxxxxxxxxxxxxxxxxxxxxxxxxxxxx

Example A. Using a fixed single unit of inter-line space
to separate each element of information has its own built-in
limitations.
   It does *not* allow for sufficient spatial distinction between:
(1) different levels of headings, or (2) levels of headings
and groups of paragraphs.

Primary heading

Secondary heading

xxxxxxxxxxxxxxxxxxxxxxxxxxxxxxxxxxxxxxxxxxxx
xxxxxxxxxxxxxxxxxxxxxxxxxxxxxxxxxxxxxxxxxxxx
xxxxxxxxxxxxxxxxxxxxxxxxxxxxxxxxxxxxxxxxxxxx

xxxxxxxxxxxxxxxxxxxxxxxxxxxxxxxxxxxxxxxxxxxx
xxxxxxxxxxxxxxxxxxxxxxxxxxxxxxxxxxxxxxxxxxxx
xxxxxxxxxxxxxxxxxxxxxxxxxxxxxxxxxxxxxxxxxxxx

Tertiary heading

xxxxxxxxxxxxxxxxxxxxxxxxxxxxxxxxxxxxxxxxxxxx
xxxxxxxxxxxxxxxxxxxxxxxxxxxxxxxxxxxxxxxxxxxx
xxxxxxxxxxxxxxxxxxxxxxxxxxxxxxxxxxxxxxxxxxxx

Example B. Combining multiples of a fixed inter-line space
gives greater spatial flexibility. It *does* allow for greater
spatial variation between: (1) different levels of headings,
and (2) levels of headings and groups of paragraphs.

Primary heading

Secondary heading

xxxxxxxxxxxxxxxxxxxxxxxxxxxxxxxxxxxxxxxxxxxx
xxxxxxxxxxxxxxxxxxxxxxxxxxxxxxxxxxxxxxxxxxxx
   xxxxxxxxxxxxxxxxxxxxxxxxxxxxxxxxxxxxxxxxx
xxxxxxxxxxxxxxxxxxxxxxxxxxxxxxxxxxxxxxxxxxxx
xxxxxxxxxxxxxxxxxxxxxxxxxxxxxxxxxxxxxxxxxxxx

Tertiary heading

xxxxxxxxxxxxxxxxxxxxxxxxxxxxxxxxxxxxxxxxxxxx
xxxxxxxxxxxxxxxxxxxxxxxxxxxxxxxxxxxxxxxxxxxx
xxxxxxxxxxxxxxxxxxxxxxxxxxxxxxxxxxxxxxxxxxxx

Example C. Has all the advantages of Example B, but
because second and subsequent paragraphs are indented
the text would take up less space.

Primary heading

Secondary heading

xxxxxxxxxxxxxxxxxxxxxxxxxxxxxxxxxxxxxxxxxxxx
xxxxxxxxxxxxxxxxxxxxxxxxxxxxxxxxxxxxxxxxxxxx
xxxxxxxxxxxxxxxxxxxxxxxxxxxxxxxxxxxxxxxxxxxx
   xxxxxxxxxxxxxxxxxxxxxxxxxxxxxxxxxxxxxxxxx
xxxxxxxxxxxxxxxxxxxxxxxxxxxxxxxxxxxxxxxxxxxx
xxxxxxxxxxxxxxxxxxxxxxxxxxxxxxxxxxxxxxxxxxxx

Tertiary heading

xxxxxxxxxxxxxxxxxxxxxxxxxxxxxxxxxxxxxxxxxxxx
xxxxxxxxxxxxxxxxxxxxxxxxxxxxxxxxxxxxxxxxxxxx
xxxxxxxxxxxxxxxxxxxxxxxxxxxxxxxxxxxxxxxxxxxx

Example D. Using multiples of half-line feeds, instead of
whole line units, gives similar results to Example B. The disadvantage of using half-line feeds is that in multiple-column
work, the lines in the columns don't always align horizontally.

Figure 9.2   Examples of the way that whole and half-line units of vertical spacing can
be used in text setting with three levels of headings.

Word spacing information
DTP Software: QuarkXpress

Word spacing units: *

Min	Opt	Max
86%	86%	86%

Character spacing units

Min	Opt	Max
0%	0%	0%

Unjustified text composition is a form of typesetting where each of the word spaces requires a *fixed* percentage unit value. This gives an uneven and 'ragged' appearance to the right-hand edge.

Unjustification allows the words at the end of the lines to remain
un-hyphenated – as the first paragraph above shows,
but if the measure is short,
it is a good idea to hypenate
words which fall within a pre-
determined hyphenation zone.

— 86% *fixed* word space set in 8.5 pt Monotype Plantin

Figure 9.3   Examples of unjustified setting.

line separation, creating uncertainty in the reader's mind and making reading more difficult. If you are using word-processing or electronic publishing software, you can select an appropriate inter-line spacing (see the manual for the package on how to do it) by experiment.

Readability rule 2   The space between lines should always be larger than the spaces between words.

* When metal type was set by hand, the compositor could use six sizes of space, as shown below. The 'thick', 'mid' and 'thin' would be used in combination to space words, and the hair space for optically spacing small capitals. Each size of type had the same proportional spaces cut to the size of that font.

EM = one
EN = half
Thick = third
Mid = quarter
Thin = fifth
Hair = 12%

In DTP programs you can specify word spaces from 1 to 400 per cent; the larger the number the wider the space. To set an equivalent to a mid space in unjustified set Plantin, would require an 86% unit fixed space.

When you have established an appropriate inter-line space, it is necessary to give further visual clues to readers with regard to proximity and grouping of textual elements and headings. It is important to be able to grasp the conceptual structure of the text and avoid ambiguity. This can be best be achieved by the use of multiples of the unit of standard inter-line space: for example by using two units of space between a heading and the sub-section under it, but three between the end of a subsection and the next heading. It easier, if you are new to typography, to set up a speci-fication to use whole line units, but half-line units can also be used (see Figure 9.2).

FORMS OF SETTING TYPE, AND SPACING BETWEEN WORDS

In text composition words should be set close together, so that the words and the lines appear to the eye to form an overall even texture. If the space between the words is too wide, then the even texture is destroyed, and the word unit becomes uneven and 'spotty' in appearance; the eye has difficulty in linking the words together, and this slows down the reading process, and in justi-fied text causes 'rivers' of white space to appear. The simplest way to achieve even word spacing is to set the text *unjustified* or ragged right, as shown in Figure 9.3.

If the text is to be *justified* correctly it is essential that:

1 The measure (line length) is neither too long nor too short.

Word spacing information
DTP Software: QuarkXpress

Examples 1 and 2

Word spacing units:

Min	Opt	Max
83%	86%	90%

Character spacing units

Min	Opt	Max
0%	0%	0%

hyphenation zone set at:
2 picas 6 pts
hyphens in a row: 2
Auto hyphenation set at:
Smallest word: 4
Maximum after: 3
Minimum after: 2

Examples 3 and 4
Set with default parameters

Word spacing units:

Min	Opt	Max
100%	100%	150%

Character spacing units

Min	Opt	Max
0%	0%	15%

hyphenation zone and
hyphens-in-a-row program:
switched off.

Figure 9.4

Justified text composition is a form of typesetting where each of the word spaces used is calculated to fit into a range of *variable* unit values. This gives a 'squared-up' left and right-hand edge, as this example shows (the bulk of the setting for this book is also justified). **Example 1**

if the measure is re-
duced to a third of
the width of the para-
graph above – and the
same typeface and
hyphenation program
is used, there are pro-
blems in some of the
lines of achieving-
close word spacing.
Example 2

if the measure is
reduced to a third of
the width of the
paragraph above –
and the same
typeface is used, but
the hyphenation
program is turned
off, it is impossible to
achieving close word
spacing. **Example 3**

Justified text composition is a form of typesetting where each of the word spaces used is calculated to fit into a range of *variable* unit values. This gives a 'squared-up' left and right-hand edge, as this example shows (the bulk of the setting for this book is also justified).
Example 4

Note: The two examples with the cross show what can happen when the default spacing parameters are turned on. Not only do you get extremely poor word spacing, but in some of the lines in Examples 3 & 4 the program inserts inter-character spacing of 15 per cent, as well as word spacing wide enough to drive a bus through.

Examples of justified setting.

2 The units of spacing between words are carefully controlled (because you can't just use one fixed percentage unit of word spacing with justification).

3 Words are hyphenated when necessary at the end of lines, in order to achieve close and even word spacing. It is usual to hyphenate no more than two consecutive lines in a row, and to specify the smallest word that you will allow to be hyphenated, plus the number of characters either side of the hyphen and the width of hyphenation zone. Unhyphenated line endings would make the word spacing uneven throughout the setting; far too wide in some lines, or too narrow in others, so making it unacceptable (see Figure 9.4).

If you are using a word-processing package you are limited in the way you can control word spacing, but with DTP programs you can select the appropriate format commands to control these

The tracking program of
DTP software can be set to
minus or *plus* unit values.

The minus unit program is
useful, if used carefully, for
reducing the overall intercharacter spacing in display
sizes, but is best **avoided**
altogether in text setting.

This is an example of justified text composition, using the same spacing program as found in Example 1 in Figure 9.4, but introducing 4 units of minus tracking.

And here is the same specification, but with 8 units of minus tracking.

This is an example of unjustified text composition, using the spacing program as specified for all the unjustified text in this book, but with 4 units of minus tracking.

And here is the same specification, but with 8 units of minus tracking.

In the first line, the type is set normally without any minus intercharacter spacing. The figure and ground is untouched, and the words are easily read.

In the second line, a small amount of minus intercharacter spacing has been specified. As a result the characters now touch, and this makes the words far more difficult to read. In text sizes the situation would be far worse.

Figure 9.5   Examples of justified and unjustified setting, with the tracking program set to minus unit values; and the effect of intercharacter spacing on the principle of figure and ground.

variables, and experiment to establish the combination that gives the best results.

SPACING BETWEEN CHARACTERS

Just as there should be close and even spacing between words, so it is also necessary to pay attention to the space between characters – especially in text setting, or when using small type at the threshold of legibility. And although DTP programs are designed to set type without the characters touching, it is only too easy to do so. If the individual characters are either touching or nearly touching, it not only slows down the pace of reading, but it also adds to eye strain by destroying the 'figure and ground' relationship (see Figure 9.5).

On the other hand, if the space between characters is too wide (see Figure 9.6 on page 140), it becomes hard to distinguish words from each other because the difference between intercharacter and inter-word spacing is too small. Once again, you can experiment with changing these variables by choosing the relevant options in whatever word-processing or electronic publishing software you are using, but these features of the program

Typographical observations

Typographical observations

Notice, in the first example on the left, how the clarity of the 'word picture' is completely destroyed when the intercharacter spacing is *opened-up* by using excessive tracking, combined with too large a word space.

Here is an example of justified text composition which uses the same type size and leading as the caption below. It has been set with the default spacing program switched on and 8 units of plus tracking specified, which is the same amount used to space the lines of small capitals in this book.

Here is the same example of unjustified text composition, using the spacing program as specified for all the unjustified text in this book, but with 6 units of plus tracking.

And here is the same specification, but with 9 units of plus tracking.

Figure 9.6

Examples of justified and unjustified text where the plus tracking program has been specified, and where the word and intercharacter spacing units are too wide.

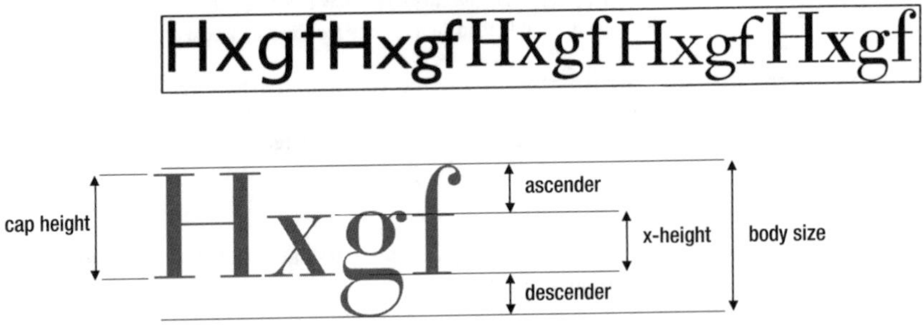

Figure 9.7

This example shows the variation in appearing size of a small number of sans serif and serif typefaces each set to 24 pts.

should be used only when you have sufficient typographic knowledge to guide the decision process.

TYPE SIZE

If you look at the type size options available in word-processing or electronic publishing software, you will see that their sizes are described in *points*. The point is a very peculiar unit! In the experience of most people, when something physical is measured – a metre of fabric, or a piece of glass – there is a direct relationship between the object and its physical dimensions. Unfortunately the same logic cannot be applied to type, for what is measured there is not the size of the type, but the full size of the 'electronic window', or the 'body size' in which it appears (see Figure 9.7).

The height of all the typefaces shown in Figure 9.7 is described as 24 points, but the only dimension that is actually 24 points is

Appearing size of type

It can be clearly seen from this sample text setting just how marked the differences in appearing size really are.

And it also shows the apparent weight or 'grey-scale' value, is influenced by the original 'in-built' design features of the font.

As we have seen from Figure 9.7 the one characteristic that influences the appearing size of type is the x-height. There are others, which influence the the final printed appearance, of the type, such as the 'index of weight' the 'index of contrast', plus the set width of the

Monotype Plantin

Adobe Garamond

Bitstream Kuenstler 480

Adobe Palatino

Bauer Bodoni

Linotype Rotation

Figure 9.8

Example of a cross-section of serif typefaces each set to 9.5 pt body size, the same point size as the text in this book.

Alphabet lengths of type

Just as the appearing size with regard to the x-height value changes in any one font, so also does the overall space taken to set the lower case alphabet. This is known as the 'set width' of the type.

abcdefghijklmnopqrstuvwxyz   Adobe Garamond
abcdefghijklmnopqrstuvwxyz   Monotype Times
abcdefghijklmnopqrstuvwxyz   Monotype Plantin
abcdefghijklmnopqrstuvwxyz   Bitstream Charter
abcdefghijklmnopqrstuvwxyz   Bitstream Kuenstler 480
abcdefghijklmnopqrstuvwxyz   Monotype New Century Schoolbook

Figure 9.9

Alphabets of a cross-section of serif typefaces each set to 9.5 pt body size.

the height of the window that surrounds the type. In fact there is very little relationship between the point size and the appearing size of any of these typefaces, and this has an important bearing on the choice of appropriate typefaces.

The one design feature above all others that influences the appearing size of any typeface is that part of the letter known as the *x-height;* this is arrived at by measuring the distance from the baseline to the top of the lower-case x. A study of a range of type-faces designed for text setting will show wide variations in this part of the typeface, and you can be fooled into thinking a type-face is a larger or smaller point size than it actually is. This can be demonstrated by looking at the lines of text type in Figure 9.8. They are all 9.5 pt, but the variation in appearing size is consider-able, making some types look twice as large as others.

Not only the x-height of letters varies between typefaces; so also does the proportion between height and width of the letters. This, as Figure 9.9 shows, is reflected in the length of the alpha-bet. Some typeface alphabets are of average width, some are

The lower the resolution of of the output device, the thicker the typeface will appear to the eye. So the appearance of any typeface will undergo considerable change of appearance at different resolution bands. **300 dpi**

The lower the resolution of of the output device, the thicker the typeface will appear to the eye. So the appearance of any typeface will undergo considerable change of appearance at different resolution bands. **600 dpi**

The lower the resolution of the output device, the thicker the typeface will appear to the eye. So the appearance of any typeface will undergo considerable change of appearance at different resolution bands. **2400 dpi**

Figure 9.10   The influence of typeface design and output resolution on the appearance of two typefaces.

wider than the average, and some are narrower. This feature is not an accident, but results from a deliberate policy of designing typefaces which can be used in solving a range of communication problems. Wide typefaces are intended for longer measures, narrow ones for use with shorter line lengths, and those of average width for measures between the extremes.

The typefaces in Figure 9.9 were designed at different times and for different technologies. Some, like Garamond, are modelled on typefaces designed as long ago as 1532, when type was made of metal and books were printed on dampened handmade paper, which had the effect of 'thickening up' the image. Others, like Bitstream Charter designed by Matthew Carter as recently as 1987, are specially designed for newspaper production where a robust letterform is essential.

TYPEFACES IN RELATION TO REPRODUCTION

In choosing typefaces, it is also necessary to take into account how the final product is to be reproduced. So far as such research products as dissertations or reports are concerned, output is today likely to be through a laser printer. Laser printer images are built up of a series of dots – usually at the fairly low resolution of 300 dots per inch (dpi), although 600 dpi is now becoming commoner. With lower-resolution printers, because there are so few dots being sampled in the text sizes, the edges and design detail of the smaller size of typeface thicken up, and the inner counters tend to fill in and lose their quality. So when using this method of output, it is important to try and select either typefaces which have been designed for printing by low-resolution laser printers, or those which do not degrade unduly. Figure 9.10 shows the difference.

Page layout for A4 dissertations and reports

General decisions about page size and orientation, about the areas that will be without print and those that will be printed, and the arrangement of the various elements of information on the page, like so much else that has been covered in this book, all need to be related to 'Who, how and what' – the readers, how they want to use the product, and the content – and the interaction between these factors.

For example, readers who have reached the age when the eye is likely to have lost some of its ability to focus on close objects (around 45) will find difficulty with continuous reading of text set to a wide measure in small typefaces with or without serifs, or those typefaces which are light or ultra-light in appearance. Anything that puts a barrier between the reader and the message obviously needs to be avoided.

With dissertations and reports, which usually have an A4 page size, the readers need to read continuously, but also, in many cases, have to scan pages to find particular pieces of information. The page layout therefore needs to be planned to make it easy for them to locate what they are looking for, as shown in the series of typographical models in Figure 9.11 on pages 144 and 145.

MARGINS
Margins are the non-printed areas of a page. They are an established part of design conventions, and take account of proportional and aesthetic values, as well as playing a part in ergonomic and technical judgement. They determine the area within which information elements are to be organized, and on the functional and ergonomic level they control the boundary of the text area, and so have a direct relation with the design decisions about such factors as type size and the number of words in a line. Figure 9.12, on page 146, shows two sets of margins appropriate for dissertations and reports.

Layout rule 1   When setting-up margins, at all times try to avoid using the **default** values which make all the margins of near equal measurement.

General observation on using A4 page sizes

The international paper size A4 is ideally suited for the design and production of dissertations and reports.

If you are a novice in design the one drawback in using A4 is that it has a ratio of $1:\sqrt{2}$, making the page size *wide* in relation to the depth.

Wide A4 pages often cause problems for the novice, frequently resulting in documents which have:
- Text areas which are overall too wide
- Type set in too small a point size
- Pages which are solid-looking and uninviting to read.

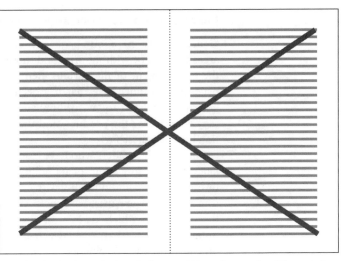

Example A Single column of text practically to the full width of the page. This layout shows you what kind of page design you get if you stick with the **default page** commands in either word processing and DTP software. You get too many words in a line for comfortable reading, margins will be proportionately too narrow, and measures too long. Type sizes will need to be between 14 & 16 pts, and the final results will be frequently uninviting to read. With some kinds of binding systems pages will not open flat.

The advantage of this kind of layout →

A single column with a wide margin to the left of the text has the advantage of:
- Giving the correct number of words to the line.
- Allowing you to use sizes of type below 14 pt, which makes it more economical on paper use.

With this layout you have to decide whether to put the extra space in each of the left-hand margins, or in the back margins. *See Example C on page 145.*

Example B Here in this A4 page the single text area has been turned into a three-column layout. This reduces the width of the text area, creating a more acceptable line length, and allowing smaller types to be used. This gives a wide left-hand margin which is ideal for secondary and tertiary headings, or side notes.

Figure 9.11   Alternative kinds of layout suitable for A4 reports and dissertations.

Notes on two loose-leaf binding systems

Spiral binders, made either of plastic or metal, allow pages to **open flat** when fixed together. Plastic comb binders are cheaper than metal spiral binders, but the life of plastic is shorter than that of metal.

Slide binders fix the individual sheets by a wedge-like plastic sleeve which slides over the sheets and forms a rigid spine. The binders are manufactured in a range of colours and spine widths. Each width is designed to take a specific number of pages.

Slide binders don't allow the sheets to **open flat**, but they are cheap to buy, and don't need special equipment.

Example C This layout is based on the same design principle of dividing the overall text area into three. This time the width of the back margins has been increased, the margins in the fore-edge have been decreased, and the two main text areas have been pushed together. This format gives wide enough back margins to use binding systems which don't allow the document to open perfectly flat. See marginal drawings.

Example D A two-column layout is used less often in the design of dissertations, but is very common in the design of reports. It is fairly easy to manage, and fits more words on to a page than the two single-column examples shown. If you want to align the text across the columns, you have to use multiples of whole units of line feed.

Figure 9.11   continued.

The parts of a double-page spread

Head margin: referred to as the 'top' margin in DTP programs.

Back margin: referred to as the 'inside' margin in DTP programs.

Trimmed edge

Fore-edge: referred to the 'outside' margin in DTP programs.

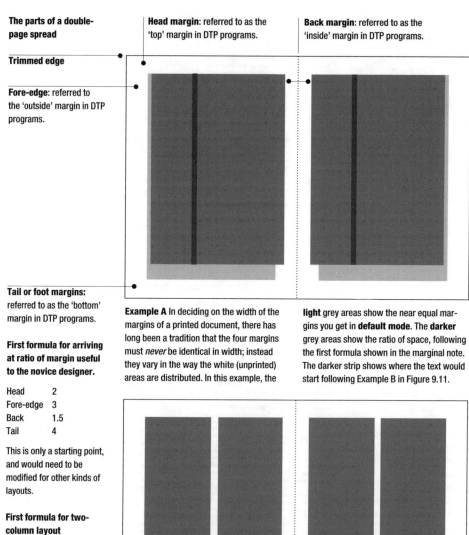

Tail or foot margins: referred to as the 'bottom' margin in DTP programs.

First formula for arriving at ratio of margin useful to the novice designer.

Head	2
Fore-edge	3
Back	1.5
Tail	4

This is only a starting point, and would need to be modified for other kinds of layouts.

First formula for two-column layout

Head	2
Fore-edge	2.5
Back	1.5
Tail	3

Note: These margins will not work for binding systems requiring a minimum back margin of 25mm.

Example A In deciding on the width of the margins of a printed document, there has long been a tradition that the four margins must *never* be identical in width; instead they vary in the way the white (unprinted) areas are distributed. In this example, the **light** grey areas show the near equal margins you get in **default mode**. The **darker** grey areas show the ratio of space, following the first formula shown in the marginal note. The darker strip shows where the text would start following Example B in Figure 9.11.

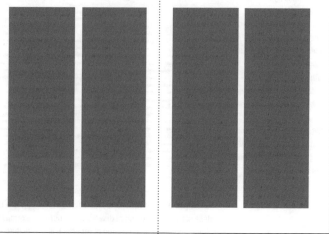

Example B In a two-column layout the proportions of the margins can be slightly changed. See the second formula shown in the margin.

Figure 9.12   Margin ratios useful for layouts using single and two-column formats.

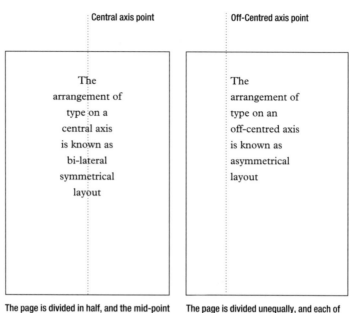

Central axis point   Off-Centred axis point

The
arrangement of
type on a
central axis
is known as
bi-lateral
symmetrical
layout

The
arrangement of
type on an
off-centred axis
is known as
asymmetrical
layout

The page is divided in half, and the mid-point of each line is positioned on the axis point.

The page is divided unequally, and each of the lines starts from an off-set axis.

Figure 9.13   The difference between bi-lateral symmetrical and asymmetrical layout.

BI-LATERAL SYMMETRY VERSUS ASYMMETRY

There are two distinct methods for arranging text on a page, symmetrical (or more accurately bi-lateral symmetrical) and asymmetrical (see Figure 9.13), although there are a few examples of printed books where the two methods are used in combination. In symmetrical layout, the type is arranged and grouped round a central axis – running vertically down the page with the mid-point of each line on the axis. In the days of manual typewriters, the typist had to spend a lot of time counting letters to find the mid-point of lines; now it is easy to select the appropriate word-processing command for symmetrical setting. The visual effect of symmetrically arranged title pages, text areas and other typographical elements is formal and visually neutral. And although symmetrically designed books or documents undoubtedly present a more formal appearance, as a visual system it is more limiting for managing complex material, and it is more difficult to read when more than a few lines are presented in this way.

Asymmetrical organization divides the page unequally; the axis is off-centre, and in its simplest form each line of type of the page starts from that axis. This form of page division allows a more flexible design approach to organizing words and graphic information, because it permits a much wider range of visual solutions. It is also one that is probably more manageable by the non-designer.

| Layout rule 2

It is advisable, as a novice learner, not to mix symmetrical and asymmetrical layout in the same document. If the text is asymmetrically organized, headings and title page should be asymmetrical too.

SELECTING AN APPROPRIATE PAGE LAYOUT

The standard page for dissertations, theses and project reports is A4. As we established in the last chapter, these products are likely to require a variety of forms of presenting information, which can make the layout of the pages quite a complex problem. As a start, Figure 9.14 shows the most frequently used layouts for an A4 format of 297 x 210 mm, annotated to indicate the types of material for which they are most suitable.

This kind of division of pages into standard areas for positioning text, illustrations, tables, etc. is called a 'grid', and arriving at a grid which will comfortably accommodate all the required information elements and help the reader to make use of them is a process to which professional designers devote a great deal of time.

Grids can be designed just for text (Figure 9.15, lower example on page 150, shows one that is similar to that designed for this book) or for text and pictures. Whatever the publication requires, the grid is a kind of ground plan, controlling where all the information elements are positioned on the page, as well as controlling their dimensions.

Once the fundamentals of grids are understood, non-designers can start to take some useful decisions for themselves, which should help them to avoid layouts that cause difficulty to readers and do not do justice to the quality of the research.

One of the most important determining factors is the amount of text that the final product is likely to contain in comparison with the number of tables and drawings to which the text has to refer. Planning of the kind described in Chapters 7 and 8 should give a fair idea of this, and of the 'worst case' that will have to be accommodated – for instance, the chapter likely to have the largest number of tables or figures. If you know that in one particular chapter which presents findings in numerical form you are going to have on average one table for every four paragraphs of text, then you know that the key problem the page layout has to

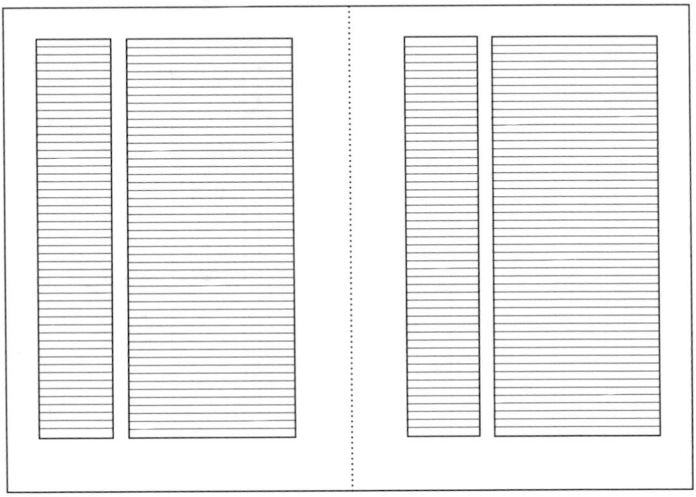

A4 double page spread, showing two un-equal columns, which are arrived at by dividing the text area by three. This layout is particularly useful for setting continuous text material, with the first column being used for secondary or tertiary headings, but it will also allow for marginal notes, or other graphic material.

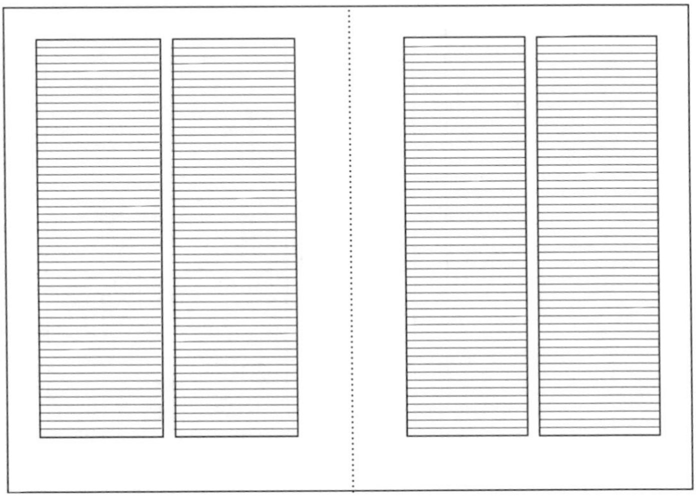

A4 double page spread, showing two equal columns of text. This layout is useful for continuous text, or a mixture of text, tables, diagrams, drawings and photographs.

Figure 9.14

Grids for text material only are calculated by taking the overall text area and dividing the depth equally into units of space These units are usually based on the type size to be used, plus the base-line to base-line measurement. So, for example, this book is based on a horizontal unit of 12 pts, which is a 9.5 pt type size added to a 2.5 pt line feed.

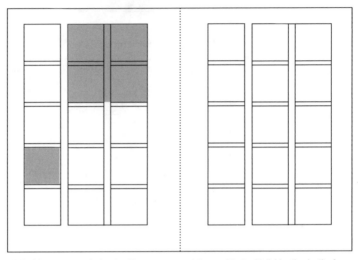

A4 double page spread, showing the same structure of two unequal columns as shown in the first example in Figure 9.14. arrived at by dividing the text area by three. This picture and text grid divides the depth of each column by the width of the measure. The smallest 'picture unit' is one square; others are multiples of these.

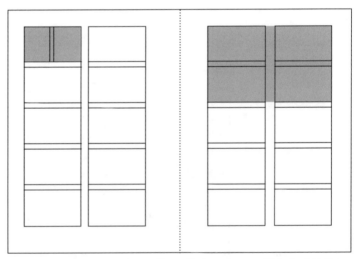

A4 double page spread, showing two equal columns. This picture and text grid divides the column depth into five equal divisions, which avoids square format pictures. The two columns could also be divided by half again, as the left-hand page of this example shows.

Figure 9.15

In each of these examples of grids, the depth of the column is divided into five divisions, with each division being equal to x-number of lines of text. The shape of the picture format is dictated by the number of columns used.

Labour productivity and labour hoarding

Male
Number (thousands)
   Percentage of total employment

Female
Number (thousands)
   Percentage of total employment

Total
Number (thousands)
   Percentage of total employment

	Male Number (thousands)	% of total employment	Female Number (thousands)	% of total employment	Total Number (thousands)	% of total employment
Mechanical engineering	842	33.2	160	20.2	1,002	30.1
Instrument engineering	102	4.0	58	7.3	160	4.8
Electrical engineering	481	18.9	282	35.5	763	22.9
Vehicles	738	29.1	116	14.6	854	16.6
All engineering	2538	100.0	794	100.0	3332	100.0

Table 4.2 **Distribution of employment by engineering orders in 1963**
Source: *Department of Employment Gazette*, March 1975

4.9 Table 4.2 shows the distribution of total engneering employment among the five orders in 1963. Mechanical engineering was the largest with one million workers or 30 per cent of engineering employment. Electrical engineering and vehicles were of roughly equal size, each employing approximately one quarter of the engineering labour force. One sixth of all engineering employment was in metal goods. In contrast, instrument engineering was comparatively unimportant, accounting for only 5 per cent of total employment. Females accounted for one quarter of the total engineering employment with instruments, electrical engineering and metal goods having the greatest concentration.

4.10 Figures 4.1-4.5 graph quarterly values of the index of production and an index of total employment from 1960(1) to 1973(3) in the five engineering orders. The indices have an average value of 100 in 1963 and, for production, we show a four quarter moving average in order to smooth out the seasonal variation over the year. The graphs use the same scale sn growth rates in different orders. Figure 4.1 shows that, for mechanical engineering, the turning points in employment coincided almost exactly with those for output. We can, however, identify two separate phases for the employment response to output changes. In the period up to the end of 1966, rapid growth in out-

put led to marked growth in total employment, while stagnant or falling output was associated with a slight decline in employment. Since the begin-ning of 1967, rapid growth in output has been associated with slow or zero growth in employment, while a declining output has resulted in a drastic reduction in the numbers employ-ed, Thus, in the eighteen months from 1970(4) the index of employment for mechanical engineering fell by some 12 per cent from 109.4 to 96.8; representing a loss of 137000 workers. (The employment decline in engineering in 1970-2 is considered in detail in Appendix A). The output decline **over** this same period was 6.5 per cent. It is quite clear that labour productivity in mechanical engineering has n much y since the beginning of 1967.

4.11 Figure 4.2 shows the output and employment indices for instruments. The distinguishing feature on the output side is the rapid growth, almost doubling in 13 years, with two periods of stagnation. The first covered most of 1966 and 1967 while the second, and more serious, has lasted for four years from the beginning of 1970. The employment index shows a generally stable level of employment in the industry. In 1973 it was the same as that observed in 1961 and there was little variation in the intervening years. The prolonged period of output stagnation at the end of the period implies a marked decline in the growth of labour produc-t

38

Figure 9.16

Example of left-hand pages from a research report showing the position of Table 4.2, with the text reference in the first paragraph below. Figures 4.1 and 4.2 appear on the opposite page. This 141-page report contained 75 separate tables and figures, but by using a mathematical distribution matrix it was possible to place all but two tables directly above, or next to, the correct page reference.

solve is 'slowing down' the flow of text so that text always appears on the same page or double-page spread as the table to which it refers – because if it doesn't, readers are going to be in difficulty and liable to get exasperated. Figure 9.16 shows the layout finally adopted for a research report which presented this problem; the text area was divided into three columns, two of which were used for text, while tables and diagrams were allowed to spread as far across the whole text area as their content required. This was enough to keep text and tables in their proper relationship; it also allowed consistency to be established in the placing of tables and diagrams – they always went at the top of the page, with the relevant text below them.

The skills that the professional typographer exercises in visually mapping information elements, and arranging them into suitable containers, are essentially a blend of the visual, the analytical and the technical. Balance is essential; if the visual form ignores the meaning and content, it can obscure them and make the reader's task harder, but on the other hand, to ignore the aesthetic will reduce the most intelligently written information to a level of banality that undermines its true quality. The fact that the visual skills required are usually given very little attention in general education contributes in no small part to the generally low standards of much printed and electronically displayed information.

Given that most of the readers of this chapter are unlikely to be designers, we end it with some reference material, that should serve as a guide to reliable ways of handling particular information elements that are likely to be needed in the information products of research. The Appendix to this chapter is a 'visual directory' to the main elements discussed in Chapter 8.

Reading list

Black, A. (1990) *Typefaces for desktop publishing: a users guide.* London: Architecture Design and Technology Press.

Kinross, R. (1992) *Modern typography: an essay in critical history.* London: Hyphen Press.

References

Orna, E. and Stevens, G (1991) Information design and information science: a new alliance? *Journal of Information Science,* (17): 197–208.

Sutnar, L. (1961) quoted in Heller, S. (1994), *Eye,* 13 (4): 44–57.

Winograd, T. and Flores, F. (1986) *Understanding Computers and Cognition. A new foundation for design.* Norwood, N. J: Ablex Publishing Corporation.

| Appendix | **Design solutions for information elements: a visual directory** |

Introduction

By accident or intention, every information product that is designed consists of a series of discrete elements, visually mapped and placed on a page. These elements are organized at two distinct levels: macro and micro.

At the macro level, each product has to have its own specific page size or 'container shape', and within that space the broad design features that give the product its own unique identity have to be visually organized into a coherent and integrated visual language.

At the micro level each separate element of information has to be placed and *visually* articulated in these areas of fixed white space by applying standard units of vertical and horizontal space. For without space, or a 'spacing scheme', the content of the message cannot be read, or even understood. See Figure 9.1a.

The 'white field'

Figure 9.1a

The 'white field' is converted into a specific page size, on which is placed each element of information. Without applying standard units of vertical or horizontal space very little sense can be made of the text information.

▌Contents page

Contents pages often present problems to the novice designer, particularly when chapter or section titles vary in the word length. The usual solution is to range the page numbers to the extreme right-hand edge of the text area, making it difficult to relate page numbers to specific titles. (See the **first half** of the example below). A far better solution is to place the page numbers at the end of the each title and separate by an EN space. (See the **second half** of the example below).

First half

Second half

Contents

■ —— EN word space

Alternative answers

Page numbers set 'full out' with full points, separated by one and two word spaces.

The word 'chapter' set in small caps, with page numbers separated from last word by an EM space followed by a solidus.

|Headings

If a report or document has a contents page, it automatically follows that you have section headings to design. Usually these primary 'A' headings are set in a larger type size – larger signifying 'more important information'. The text itself often has a further three levels of headings, B, C and D, and the example below shows two possible answers to the treatment of headings. It is necessary to design the opening chapter with an 'opening drop' allowing sufficient space between 'A' headings and the start of the text.*

'A' heading set in a larger type size than the body text.
* The grey tinted area shows the 'chapter drop'.

'B' headings set in the bold font of the text size.

'C' headings set in the small caps of the text font, with 20 units of tracking.

'D' headings set in the italic font of the text.

Note: Because this is a single column of text, the line spaces used to separate headings from the previous paragraph are based on whole and half line units.

---

1   What are we doing when we 'do research'?

Transformations and the cycle of communication

I have just spoken of 'transforming' knowledge into an 'information product'. *Transformation* is a key concept which underlies everything I have to say in this book, so let me give a basic explanation of what I mean when I apply it to *information* and *knowledge*.

The long history of the development of the human mind and of our power to think and communicate with one another is really a history of transformations.

THE FIRST TRANSFORMATION

The development of the human mind started when the first humans transformed their experience of the outside world into representations of it inside their minds. What set them apart from the apes was their way of doing this.

The first step
The first step in that process was what Merlin Donald (1991) calls 'visugraphic invention' – the symbolic use of graphic devices. This began about 40,000 years so (Australian aboriginal rock carvings and paintings, for

14

Alternative treatment

'C' headings in italic

'D' headings in roman, combined with a square, followed by an EN space

---

The first transformation

The development of the human mind started when the first humans transformed their experience of the

■ The first step
The first step in that process was what Merlin Donald (1991) calls 'visugraphic invention' – the symbolic use

❙ Coding of paragraphs

The conventions most frequently used to signal a new paragraph are the indent and the separation of paragraphs by a line space. There are other codes that can be used, for instance ¶ or ⸿ can occasionally be found in use, but the indent or the line space – or a proportion of it – is the most common.

One advantage of the indent is that there can be no doubt as to where the paragraph starts. If paragraphs are set 'full out' there is bound to be a percentage of paragraphs that will make a 'full line', resulting in no spatial clues that the next line is in fact a new paragraph. For this reason alone, coding paragraphs this way is always best avoided.

Comments on the setting

No indents or line space. This method relies on the last line of each paragraph always falling short of the measure. In this example a new paragraph begins 'Besides the human eye … but this is effectively obscured by the way the lines fall, so this method of paragraph coding is best avoided.

Times for quiet reading have become rare. The large amount of printed text which we have to work through daily compels us to read hastily, a fact that is not always considered. Many of our newspapers and periodicals present hindrances to fluent reading. There is, for example often a lack of distinction between information, news and supplementary commentary. Besides the human eye there is, today, the electronic eye of the reading machines. For these machines, letters are not a problem of form but a problem of distinction, if we are to keep the amount of reading mistakes low in order to justify the use of these very expensive machines.
HERMANN ZAPF *About Alphabets*. The MIT Press, 1970.

A single line space to separate paragraphs clearly indicates the start of each paragraph. The only disadvantage is the point mentioned in the introductory section about splitting paragraphs at the end of a page, or column.

Times for quiet reading have become rare. The large amount of printed text which we have to work through daily compels us to read hastily, a fact that is not always considered. Many of our newspapers and periodicals present hindrances to fluent reading. There is, for example often a lack of distinction between information, news and supplementary commentary.

Besides the human eye there is, today, the electronic eye of the reading machines. For these machines, letters are not a problem of form but a problem of distinction, if we are to keep the amount of reading mistakes low in order to justify the use of these very expensive machines.
HERMANN ZAPF *About Alphabets*. The MIT Press, 1970.

First paragraph full out, and subsequent paragraphs indented one EM of the type size. This is the most common method of indicating the start of a paragraph.

Times for quiet reading have become rare. The large amount of printed text which we have to work through daily compels us to read hastily, a fact that is not always considered. Many of our newspapers and periodicals present hindrances to fluent reading. There is, for example often a lack of distinction between information, news and supplementary commentary.
    Besides the human eye there is, today, the electronic eye of the reading machines. For these machines, letters are not a problem of form but a problem of distinction, if we are to keep the amount of reading mistakes low in order to justify the use of these very expensive machines.
HERMANN ZAPF *About Alphabets*. The MIT Press, 1970.

Paragaphs or lists

This page deals with a range of typograph-ical answers, associated with the numbering of paragraphs, and other sub-problems of text and the coding of lists

Numbered paragraphs

Example 1. The numbers are separated from the start of the text by an EM space.

Example 2. Single paren-thesis, with an EM space.

Example 3. Here only a word space is used, and that does not provide sufficient space to separate the numbers from the text.

1.1 Research reports – or similar kinds of documentation – often re-quire that paragraphs are numbered sequentially using decimal numbers.
Example 1

1.2) With decimal numbers the first digit indicates the chapter number, the second the paragraph. The value of paragraph numbering is that it allows any parts of the document to be referred to quickly and accurately.
Example 2

1.3 If numbered paragraphs are not part of the typographical problem, then numbered or coded lists well might be.
Example 3

Numbered statements

Example 4. Numbered statements – or itemised lists – can be treated in a similar way to paragraphs. But, unlike a paragraph number, lists can create problems if they exceed more than one line.

Example 5. The solution to this problem is to indent all subsequent lines.

1 Text separated from the number by an EN space.
2 If on the other hand some of the statements in the list exceed a single line, the numbers will tend to disappear into the gen-eral texture of the setting.
3 As soon as lines that 'turn over' are indented, the numbers become clearer, and can then be scanned with ease.
Example 4

1 Text separated from the number by an EN space.
2 If on the other hand some of the statements in the list exceed a single line, the numbers will tend to disappear into the gen-eral texture of the setting.
3 As soon as lines that 'turn over' are indented, the numbers become clearer, and can then be scanned with ease.
Example 5

Emphasizing lists

Other techniques of treating and emphasizing lists.

If it is important to distinguish each item in a list, but not to number, this can be achieved by using some form of coding. The most common is a bullet point, but it could be a square, or a triangle.
- a bullet point set two sizes down from the text size.
- a solid square, set two sizes down from the text size.
- a triangle, set two sizes down from the text size.

Emphasizing words within continuous text

It is often necessary to signal to the reader a change of emphasis, to make a point more emphatically, or to explain particular facets of text. To achieve this you can:
- use *italic,* or slanting roman
- use **bold** at the same size, or in some cases in a **larger** size
- use SMALL CAPITALS with tracking
- or use a contrasting **type** face

Cross-references

It is often necessary to refer the reader to a particular page, or a series of pages, from any point in a document.

This forwards or backwards navigation can be achieved by words only, or by adding graphic codes to the words.

Using words and symbols

Roman or italic and old face figures, enclosed by parentheses.

Indice (printers fist) combined with words, enclosed by square brackets.

The implications of collections management policies for access via catalogues and the national bibliographic service have already been considered (see pages 145 and 146).
… reconsideration which affected policies for both acquisition (*see below, pages 151 –153*) and cataloguing.
… 'by staff at appropriate levels' [☞ see p83]. In reality, the situation demands the use of professional judgement and experience to ensure that 'the consequences are clearly understood and publicised, and to readjust … policies accordingly.' [☞ *see* p 84].

Tables

The design of tables is an interesting problem, and one that is often given very little thought. Basically there are two typographical conventions used for setting tables. The first is to place boxes around the primary pieces of information, and then to place the entire table in a larger rectangle. The second, which is much simpler to do, is to remove the vertical rules, and use only horizontal rules.

Using rules of the same width, and placing the headings in the centre of the box. Note that lining figures have been used which are less confusing to read in tables than old face – or non-lining figures.

Occupational group	Conventional route		NC route	
	No. of manhours	% of total	No. of manhours	% of total
1 Technician & above	0	0	0	0
2 Craftsmen plus	1950	21	860	38
3 Craftsmen	6872	76	412	19
4 Operators & others	268	3	965	43
Total	**9090**	**100**	**2237**	**100**

Using horizontal rules only, and ranging the headings on a left or right axis, and the figures on a right axis.

Occupational group	Conventional route		NC route	
	No. of manhours	% of total	No. of manhours	% of total
1 Technician & above	0	0	0	0
2 Craftsmen plus	1950	21	860	38
3 Craftsmen	6872	76	412	19
4 Operators & others	268	3	965	43
Total	**9090**	**100**	**2237**	**100**

Flow diagrams

Flow diagrams are a useful device for structuring information and helping the reader to understand a sequence of events. They are especially useful when alternative courses of action are involved, because the reader can be directed to the appropriate one by responding YES or NO to questions. Their very nature, however, means that they can easily come to look visually disorganised

It is important that the overall layout of flow diagrams relates to any other visual elements within the document, and consideration is given to:

- the weight of all the lines and boxes
- the size and weight of the typefaces used
- the way the information reads
- the size and kind of arrow used.

It is possible to remove the boxes altogether if the information is straightforward and not too complex in its sequence.

Positioning of lines and arrows does become a problem, if the routes through the information become too complex or too numerous.

Boxes and arrow heads

Lines and arrow heads of the same thickness. Arrows positioned short of the adjacent box.

Thicker lines, and visually heavier arrows used without connecting lines. Note: this method can be used only if all the boxes are placed near to each other.

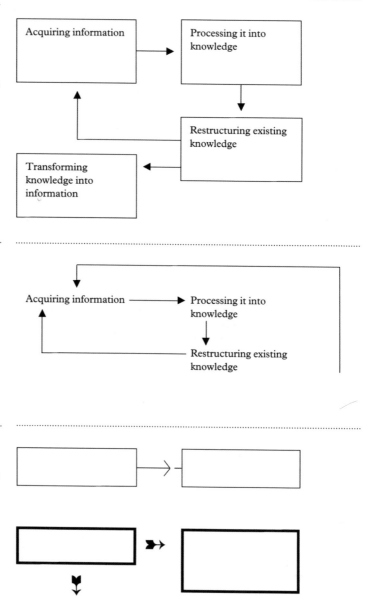

Distinguishing text

As all typography is concerned with making language visual, it is frequently required that some aspects of a text are emphasized, or coded in some particular way. By this I don't mean the occasional word set in italic – which has been dealt with on page 157 – but the extension of display typography more commonly found in magazine design.

Example 1. There were a number of elements in this book which needed to have a different appearance from the main text. In was solved like this: 'definitions' appeared as a marginal note, and set in small caps, the text was set in italic, and words requiring to stand out were set in roman.

Example 2. Another element which needed to 'differ' from the main text. Here the same corner rules were used, only this time placed within the main text area, where the main text face was replaced by a condensed sans serif type.

DEFINITIONS

Knowledge and information

Knowledge *is what we acquire from our interaction with the world; it is the result of experience organized and stored inside each individual's own mind in a way that is unique to each (though there are features common to how we all do it). It comes in two main kinds: knowledge* about *things, and* know-how. *We make it our own by* transforming *the experience that comes from outside into internal knowledge.*

Antonio Crestadoro (1856) made a wise observation about the consequence as they affected readers in the British Museum Library over a century ago:

Freedom is, in all things, an essential condition of growth and power. The purpose of readers in search of a book are as manifold as the names and subjects, or headings under which the book may be traced. Entering the book only once is giving but one of its many references and suppressing the remainder.

His solution was to enter a shorthand version of the book's details under *all* the relevant headings, in a kind

Index

Indexes are usually designed to fit either a two or three column grid, and are a straightforward enough problem, particularly if the majority of entries will fit on to a single line, with only the occasional word/s turning over. But if the index has more than one level of information, or changes in typographical coding, then this will require more careful attention to the overall design detail.

Example 1. Single line entries, with lines that don't fit the measure being 'turned over' and indented one EM of the type size. Page numbers are separated from text by an EM space.

Example 2. Where there is more than one level of information, the easiest way is to 'visually show' this second level by indenting by an EM space.

Example 3. Shows EN dashes replacing some of the indents.

Previews

It is often a good idea to design the main chapter openings as a separate page, and add a preview, which is really a second-ary kind of contents page.

This one is just a bulleted list, which follows the same typographical style as is used in the design of the text pages.

6 Developing the policy

In this chapter
- Identifying the key points that the policy should cover
- The basic objectives of an information policy
- Presenting the policy to top management and to those who will develop it and implement it
- Selecting key areas for further policy development, and drawing in the people most concerned to work on it
- Starting points for implementation

Summaries

Summaries, like previews, are useful in recapitulating the main features of a chapter. This one is just a straightforward list, which follows the same typo-graphical style as the chapters themselves.

Summary

An object can be in only one place at a time.

In order to think about it in relation to other objects it is necessary to represent it in such a way that the representation can be freely moved about.

The representation is a record which gives essential details of the object.

Records are one of the essential parts of any system of handling information. They are the inputs to the system, and what is not included in them cannot be retrieved and output.

Footnotes

Footnotes are frequently a vital element in any document or report, and, like every other topic in this 'visual directory', they need to be treated as a design problem.

Footnotes – as the name implies – nor-mally appear at the 'foot' of the page, and are usually set in two sizes smaller than the text size. Alternatively, if the page design gives wide back margins, footnotes can become marginal notes and be positioned in this area of the page.

The text references to any footnote are usually signalled numerically from 1 to n, and in a point size smaller than the text size. In some text fonts these numerals are specially designed and supplied separately, as 'expert sets'.

8. From the Bauhaus letterheading (1925) designed by Herbert Bayer and reproduced in Tschichold, *Die neue Typographie*, p.128.

The main lesson taken by the typographers from *Sprache und Schrift* was the idea of the simplified one-alphabet orthography of 'Kleinschreibung', in which 'our letters lose nothing, but rather become more legible, easier to learn, essentially more scientific'.[8]

8. From the Bauhaus letterheading (1925) designed by Herbert Bayer and reproduced in Tschichold, *Die neue Typographie*, p.128.

10 | Transforming knowledge into written information: designing your writing

The final transformation

The first chapter of this book spoke of transformation as 'a key concept which underlies everything I have to say', and identified it as a two-way process. In the early stages of research, the main kind of transformation is of information from the outside world into knowledge in the mind. When we come to the actual writing of the final product, we are embarking on the second direction of transformation: turning the knowledge we have gained during the research back into information in the outside world in the form of an information product. This is a peculiarly difficult process. Unfortunately people who are doing it for the first time very often don't realize how hard it is until too late.

A design approach to writing

The approach recommended here can be described as 'sneaking up on writing' – taking a step-by-step approach which gets some of the major decisions out of the way before we begin to write, so that our minds are left free to concentrate on what is surely one of the most difficult tasks that human beings have set themselves (see page 172 for why writing is such a difficult activity). This chapter looks in particular at the activities involved in getting information out of store and transforming it into an effective written product, and at the proportions of time they require. It suggests simple and practical ways of handling the information we want to use in writing, and gives examples of a 'design approach' to the actual writing – that is, one which plans the end product to meet the needs of those who will use it, seeks a strong and elegant structure appropriate to those needs and to the nature of the content, and draws on options for presenting the elements of information which fit both users' needs and the content. The metaphor which fits this approach is perhaps that of creating 'containers' or frameworks into which we can write, as opposed to that of weaving or knitting words into a long strip and then cutting it up and stitching it together to make into a product, which is what the usual process of writing suggests.

The emphasis is on preparing the mind for writing so that we start with clear knowledge of how the information is going to be presented, and so are free to give full attention to purely writing problems. The transition from preparatory activities, which in themselves involve some writing anyway, to writing the final product, will then be just one more step in a logical process, and so the words are likely to be well chosen, and the style of presentation appropriate to the content and the reader. If the preparation has not been thorough, no amount of detailed advice about sentence length, grammatical points, syntax or choice of words is going to be of much use. It is a weakness of many of the texts that purport to help people with writing that they concentrate on telling their readers to use short words to keep their 'fog index' [1] low, or advising them to introduce a point of interest 'approximately every 500 words' and to finish 'on a high point which leaves the reader breathless', while paying only lip-service to the need to organize information and relate its presentation to the readers and the use to be made of it.

Tools to take the stress out of writing

If you have followed the steps suggested in earlier chapters you will have built up a set of powerful tools that will take much of the stress out of writing. This is what you will have:

- An organized store of materials relevant to the research, together with your own notes (see Chapter 3).
- A set of 'keys' that lets you get into the store and find whatever is relevant to particular topics (see Chapter 3).
- Documentation on the progress of the research, the methods adopted, and the 'instruments' used in applying them (see Chapter 4).

---

[1] The 'fog index' is one of a number of 'readability formulas' that have been devised to assess how easy text is to read. The basis for it is the length of sentence and length of words – a somewhat unbalanced criterion; as Sides (1982: E-107) points out 'language is non-existent devoid of its context, and this is where readability formulas fail. They tend to make writers think of writing without a context, without an audience'. The same can be said of the exclusive reliance on 'plain English' to solve problems of communication; to do so is to 'concentrate on the transmission of information rather than on the dynamics of how people communicate' (Shulman and Sless, 1994: 70), to seek to control content, rather than to manage the relationship between the information product and its readers.

- Top-level decisions on the structure and sequence of the final product – an outline contents list (see Chapter 7).
- Provisional decisions about forms of presentation for different kinds of content – the information elements you will need – and standards for them (see Chapters 8 and 9).
- Provisional decisions on a visual structure of the page – the page layout – which will be appropriate for the product (see Chapter 9).

You will in fact have built up a quite detailed specification for the product you are about to write, and a set of standards for the different elements you will use, as well as an accessible body of information to draw on. Figure 10.1 shows this in graphic form, and indicates how it can contribute to the writing.

Before you start to write

For those of us who feel daunted by writing, the more problems we take care of before starting and the more of our ideas we are able to place 'outside in the world' for inspection before we start, the better the process is likely to go. And even for those who actually like writing, the quality of the end product will be improved by pre-planning and visualizing. Everything that I recommend here is based on things I have found out for myself or learned from colleagues and students; and a lot of it has been tried out by other researchers, who have made their own adaptations and found them useful. These are some basic steps that should be helpful.

LABEL YOUR MATERIALS

As a first step, take the outline contents list (see Chapter 7, pages 108–109). With that beside you, go through the store of information you have collected, and your own notes, and label every item with the chapter number or section title to which it is relevant. If you have recorded the items in your collection in a computer database (see Chapter 3, page 52), you can add the relevant chapter numbers to the records, so that you can easily find everything you need to refer to for a given chapter. Figure 10.2, on page 166, shows an example.

Then you can do the same with the documentation which you have developed about the research (see Chapter 4); that should provide the basis for a chapter or section on the methodology used in the research, and will also be useful for pointers to key findings and conclusions. It can also be helpful in refreshing the

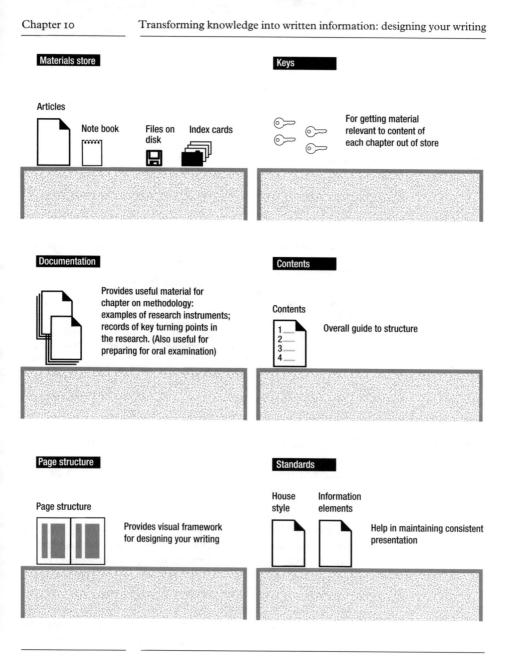

Figure 10.1   Tools to take the stress out of writing.

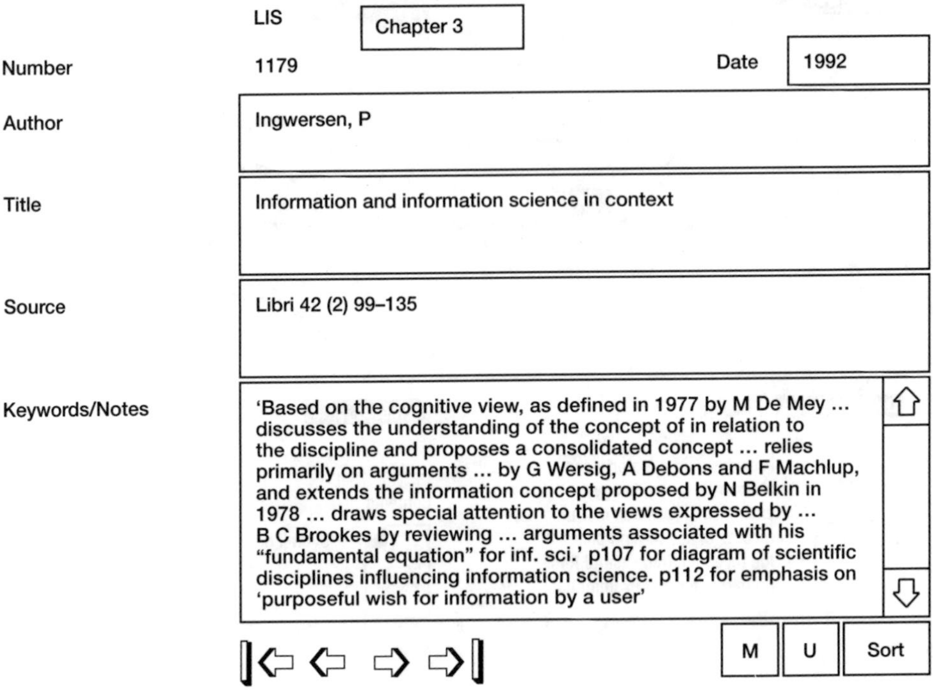

	LIS	Chapter 3
Number	1179	Date 1992
Author	Ingwersen, P	
Title	Information and information science in context	
Source	Libri 42 (2) 99–135	

Keywords/Notes

'Based on the cognitive view, as defined in 1977 by M De Mey … discusses the understanding of the concept of in relation to the discipline and proposes a consolidated concept … relies primarily on arguments … by G Wersig, A Debons and F Machlup, and extends the information concept proposed by N Belkin in 1978 … draws special attention to the views expressed by … B C Brookes by reviewing … arguments associated with his "fundamental equation" for inf. sci.' p107 for diagram of scientific disciplines influencing information science. p112 for emphasis on 'purposeful wish for information by a user'

⬆ ⬇

|⇐ ⇐ ⇒ ⇒| M   U   Sort

Figure 10.2   Label items with the chapter number to which they are relevant.

memory and developing ideas for any oral examination or presentation on the research.

STANDARDS FOR REFERENCE

Next, put together examples of the standards you have decided on for the information elements you plan to use, and a copy of the 'house style' you will use for such recurring elements as references, authors' names, etc. (see Chapters 8 and 9). They will act as 'external memory' to help in maintaining consistency of presentation. If you get it right first time you can save a lot of tedious work and a lot of time later on. I say this feelingly, because in writing this book I neglected to keep beside me the publisher's standards, and, after the first chapter, forgot the proper style for references, and the fact that 'z' rather than 's' spelling was required. It took me a few hours that could have been better spent to remedy the deficiency.

Human beings are not good at being consistent, and need all the help they can get in achieving it.

A FIRST STORYBOARD

A 'storyboard' is a useful first step towards the 'visual framework' for writing. The method comes from the motion picture industry, and is also used in the design of illustrated books, but it is a useful device for the writer of informative products too. It gives a 'working model' in the form of a series of pages or double-page spreads, and allows you to decide in outline what each needs to tell the reader. In the first instance, each 'page' can represent a chapter or main section from the contents list. Working with physically separate pages makes it easier to decide the overall sequence; as they are separate, you can group them in different ways, and easily swap round the order of different sections or groups of sections until you are satisfied you have the one that will be most helpful to readers. Figure 10.3a, on page 168, shows an example.

Storyboarding also helps with seeing the places where readers will need help in getting from one set of ideas or topic to the next. When you have arranged the separate elements of the storyboard in what seems a good sequence, look at them to see the places where you will need to help your readers with a 'bridge' from one section to another and mark the places where bridges are needed (see Figure 10.3b on page 168).

ORGANIZING THE MATERIAL FOR INDIVIDUAL CHAPTERS

Now you can think about organizing the themes of the individual chapters. Here a similar approach to the one suggested in Chapter 7 (Figure 7.3) for organizing the main themes of the dissertation into a contents list can be useful (see also Figure 8.2).

1 Scatter the main themes or topics on a sheet of paper, so that those most closely associated are near to each other, or put each on an individual card so that they can be moved around.

2 Draw the connecting links.

3 Number the themes to show the sequence and hierarchy.

4 Organize them into a contents list for the chapter.

5 Finally, give each theme an identifying colour or shape code, which can be used to mark material relevant to the themes in notes, etc., as shown in Figure 10.4 on page 169.

Then you can put together the notes and items from your collection which you will need for the chapter, and mark them to show which themes they relate to. Figure 10.5, on page 170, shows a page of notes marked like this.

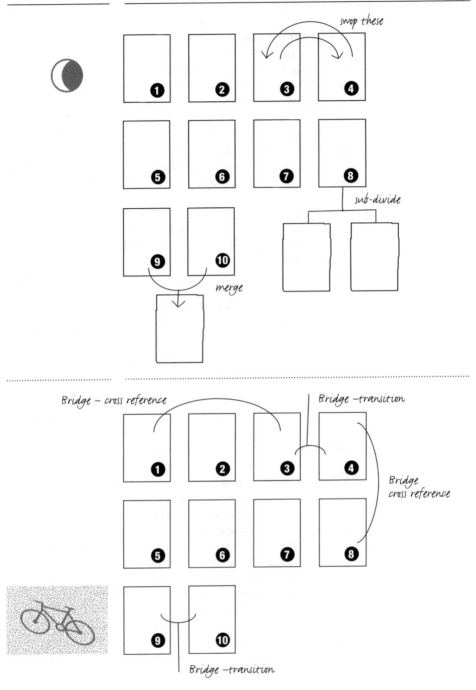

Figure 10.3a and b   Top: a storyboard helps to get the sequence right. Bottom: a storyboard with 'bridges' marked.

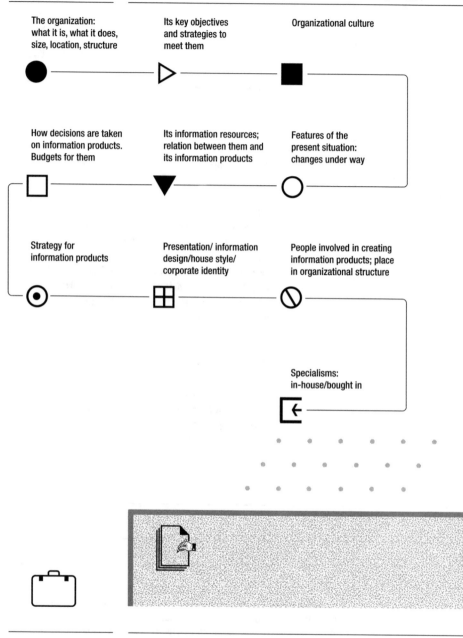

The organization:
what it is, what it does,
size, location, structure

Its key objectives
and strategies to
meet them

Organizational culture

How decisions are taken
on information products.
Budgets for them

Its information resources;
relation between them and
its information products

Features of the
present situation:
changes under way

Strategy for
information products

Presentation/ information
design/house style/
corporate identity

People involved in creating
information products; place
in organizational structure

Specialisms:
in-house/bought in

Figure 10.4   Part of a diagram of themes for a chapter, showing 'coding' of topics.

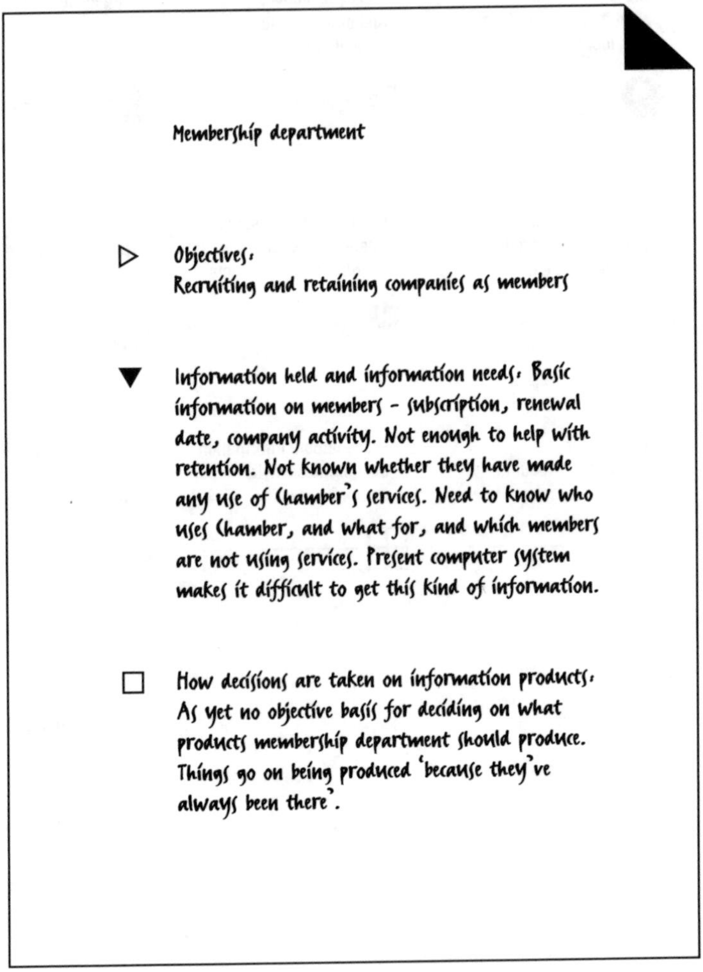

Membership department

▷ Objectives:
   Recruiting and retaining companies as members

▼ Information held and information needs: Basic
   information on members – subscription, renewal
   date, company activity. Not enough to help with
   retention. Not known whether they have made
   any use of Chamber's services. Need to know who
   uses Chamber, and what for, and which members
   are not using services. Present computer system
   makes it difficult to get this kind of information.

☐ How decisions are taken on information products:
   As yet no objective basis for deciding on what
   products membership department should produce.
   Things go on being produced 'because they've
   always been there'.

Figure 10.5   Using the coding of themes to mark relevant sections of notes from
                         case study interviews in a Chamber of Commerce.

Note: There are various options for coding notes. For purposes of
illustration in this book, computer-generated symbols have been used,
but for day-to-day purposes I use colour-coding of handwritten or
printed-out notes with highlighter pens. It is also possible to use hand-
drawn symbols, or to incorporate computer-generated symbols into
word-processed files (they should be simple-to-make ones in that case).

MINIATURE PAGE LAYOUTS

The next stage is to develop a detailed visual framework for the individual chapter in the form of a series of double-page spreads. This is the point at which all the decisions taken earlier about content, forms of presentation and visual standards converge and enrich one another. A quotation from some notes about using this method for a book will explain how to apply it and why it is useful:

> The next step was to 'design my writing' more deeply. Writing this book gave me the opportunity of applying on a large scale a method which I owe originally to an experiment by Graham Stevens. It helped him, as a designer, to apply a 'design approach' to the task of writing. It has helped me, as a writer without design training, to overcome many of my previous problems in writing. I have passed it on to a good number of design and other students in the last few years, and they too have found it helpful. Before actually starting to write each chapter, I expanded the storyboard for it into a number of rough double-page spreads, with text area and margins proportional to the designer's decision on page structure. I wrote on each spread the headings under which I planned to write, and indicated the different kinds of 'information element' I thought would be useful. I also used the spreads to remind myself of the notes and references I wanted to draw on in writing.
>
> It was only when I had a set of such spreads for a chapter, accompanied by a small heap of notes and references arranged in the sequence in which I wanted to use them, that I felt ready to start actually writing. And I can confirm from the experience that what I have so often told students is really true for me – having a visual framework to 'write into' and everything relevant ready to hand makes the complex and difficult activity of writing truly manageable and actually enjoyable. This is something I think I should never have arrived at without the experience of working with typographic designers and seeing how they make knowledge visible by placing it outside the mind in a structured form.

Figure 10.6 shows an example.

Put with each set of layouts for the chapter the materials you need to draw on – notes, copies of articles (see page 174 for making good use of them).

SET THE PAGE FORMAT FOR YOUR WORK

If you are using word-processing or desktop publishing software, set top, bottom and side margins, spacing, font and type size for the product, in line with your design decisions (see Chapter 9, pages 134 to 146). If you are using a manual or electric type-

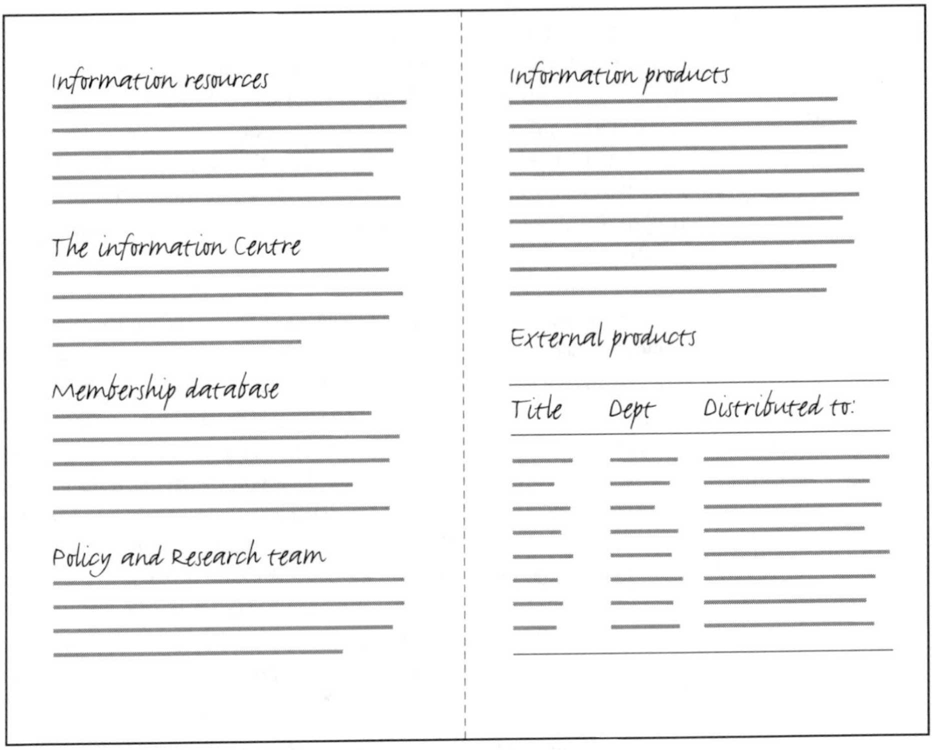

Figure 10.6   Miniature rough page layouts for a section of the case study report

writer, draw the text area as a template to ensure consistent head and foot margins, and set the side margins.

The business of writing

At last! Why is writing so difficult? It is probably because, while writing is a necessary instrument, it is an imperfect one; it had to be invented, but it puts the human mind through a lot of hoops. In part it is because the transformation of knowledge in the mind to information in the outside world requires us to turn a dynamic, constantly changing, 'three-dimensional' structure in which everything is simultaneously present, into a static, two-dimensional one, using, for the most part, words which have to be put down one at a time in linear strings. This in itself may be one of the reasons why an intermediate visual stage appears to be helpful. And there is perhaps a historic precedent; as Merlin Donald (1991)

tells us, 'visugraphic invention' – the symbolic use of graphic devices as in the cave paintings of Lascaux and Altamira – was a
step on the long path from speech to writing (the process of creating speech took hundreds of thousands of years, but by 50,000
years ago it had developed among the humans who were our direct ancestors; advanced graphic skills appeared in Europe 25,000
years ago; and writing a mere 6,000 years ago, in Mesopotamia).

These are some of the things that I have found most helpful.

DON'T COPY-TYPE!

Try to do as much of the actual writing as possible at the keyboard; it takes practice, but once you have gained the confidence
to try it, it's liberating, and it saves time. It is a poor use of time to
write everything in longhand and then copy-type it – even if you
are very fast at keyboarding, it will add half as much again to the
time spent on writing. But if it's helpful to draft outlines or difficult sentences by hand, then do it.

So far as I can judge from asking the post-graduate students I
come across, not many of them can type fast; most describe their
typing as slow or very slow (unlike students in the USA, for
whom it's not a problem because they learned at school). It is
really worthwhile to learn to touch-type; if you can use all your
fingers with some assurance of hitting the right keys instead of
pecking uncertainly around the keyboard with two fingers, not
only will typing take you less than half the time, it will also be less
fatiguing.

The other advantage of being able to compose direct on screen
is that it frees you from the discouragement of crossing out, dis-
carding false starts and seeing a growing heap of crumpled bits of
paper around the waste-paper basket. If you are word-processing,
you can quietly dispose of a phrase you don't like, you can easily
move sentences and paragraphs around, and there is no tedious
rewriting and no discarded drafts.

A HOOK TO HANG WRITING ON

Something I learned recently was the idea of writing an introductory paragraph for each chapter, once I had decided on the outline contents list. It happened because the publisher wanted to
give the introductory paragraphs to the people who were referee-
ing the proposal for this book, and I discovered that it provided
me with a useful 'hook' to hang the rest of the chapters from as I
came to writing them.

'WRITING IN LAYERS'

Even with all these preparatory stages, it is usually still a strain to try to go straight into the finished version of a chapter. Something I find useful – I have applied it in writing this book – is to start by inputting the headings for the chapter, coding them to show the hierarchy, like this:

\<B head\>
Before you start to write

\<C head\>
Label your materials

Then I draft what I want to say in note form under each heading, using the rough page sketches as guide. The next step is to print out the chapter as it now stands, and make notes on it about how to develop the sections; then I go back into the file to develop the notes into a final draft of the text. The process is a kind of 'growing the writing from seed', or building it in successively more detailed layers (see Figure 10.7 on page 175).

NOTES AND QUOTES – MAKING THE BEST OF THE SOURCES

Most research requires a lot of time spent in studying the work and findings of other people in the field, locating material relevant to the researcher's own project, sorting data and ideas into their key strands, and evaluating them. When we come to write our own research, we have to draw on that work. We need to be clear in the first place *why* we do it. It is not just to show our acquaintance with authors of whom our tutors seem to think highly. The real purposes are to:

1 Show that we have managed to find sources relevant to what we're doing, and haven't missed the key ones.
2 Show we have found and understood in them points of particular significance for our own project.
3 Use them to illuminate or support our ideas, or as a point of departure if we think otherwise.
4 Give a meaningful analysis of the range of sources we have used, so as to reveal the main trends, different schools of thought, or indeed the lack of attention to our own chosen area of research.

This can be the dreariest part of the whole proceedings for both writer and reader, but it need not be. It is one of the points where the process of constant reviewing of material and documentation of research (see Chapter 4) can pay off handsomely. If you build up your analysis of what you are getting from your

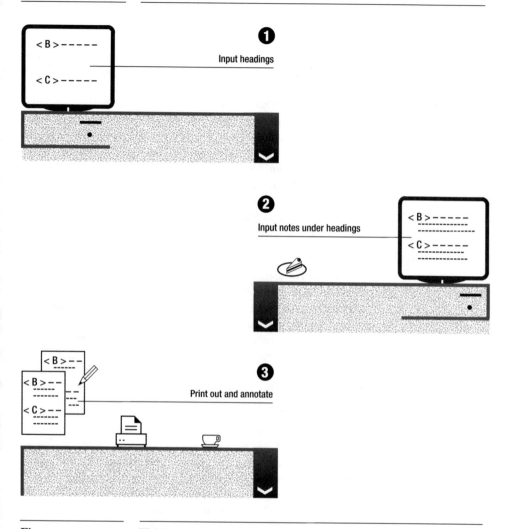

Figure 10.7   Writing in layers.

sources as the work goes forward, it makes it easier to write this part of the final product.

Probably the worst way of handling the sources is the traditional 'literature review' of the kind that appears in 'review articles', where everything is flattened down into continuous prose, and it is difficult to get a clear vision of the main ideas and who is responsible for them. If there are certain sources which have provided the basic orientation for your research, acknowledge them at the beginning. If studying the sources was an essential preliminary to deciding on the field of your research, you will need to give them a chapter or section near the start, so that readers can see what influenced you and judge its validity. In that case, organize your sources under headings that relate to your themes, and summarize what they contribute.

Be selective about quotations; make sure that they are truly relevant to the context in which you are placing them, keep them short, and use them when they give a sharper expression of a particular idea than any paraphrase in your own words would give. And as soon as you have inserted a quotation in your text, put the reference to it in the reference list. (For this reason, if you have a choice, it's easier to group references at the end of chapters, rather than putting them all into one large set at the end of the dissertation; it is also easier on the reader to be able to find details of a source by turning to the end of the chapter.)

PRINT OUT OFTEN!

While writing direct on screen is useful, it's not easy to get an overview of what the chapter is looking like. So, print out frequently so that you can spread out the pages and see what you've got, and whether you're being consistent. (I had problems with writing the last three chapters of this book – they were done on a laptop computer without facilities for printing; the surroundings were very quiet and conducive to writing, but it was not so easy to review what I had written.)

USING TIME WISELY; FINDING THE RIGHT PACE

Writing the final product is probably the most stressful part of whole business of research, and one of the most tiring of activities. So allow plenty of time for it, don't try to do too much at a stretch, and break it down into stages – repeated passes are easier than trying to get to the finished version straight away. All the approaches to writing recommended in this chapter are designed to help in using time wisely and to reducing the strain of writing. Do the most demanding things at the time of day or night when you have highest levels of thinking power; use the other times for more mechanical sorting and checking jobs. (The advice in Chapter 5 on using time, scheduling, and avoiding stress is particularly important when you reach this stage.)

One of the things that usually takes researchers by surprise is the amount of time it takes to bring the final product to the standard required before it can be handed in. Such things as ensuring consistency between chapter headings in the contents list and the form in which they appear in text, correct pagination, fitting in the right page numbers to cross-references, checking the style of references and verifying that each text reference is covered in the reference list, take a great deal of time. All too often that time is not available because it hasn't been allowed for, and so the dissertation or report goes in with a lot of imperfections. Unfortunately, although they are trivial in themselves, they quickly become apparent to examiners as they move about the text, and not only are they exasperating because they make it hard to cross-check and verify, they also cast doubt on the integrity and care of the whole research. One starts to ask oneself, 'If they can't get the surface things right, how do I know if I can trust anything they say?'

Table 10.1 shows the approximate proportions of time required for the various activities that go into writing.

Be your own editor

A final responsibility for researchers is to be the editor of their own work; you can't rely on anyone else being able or willing to cast a critical and meticulous eye over the presentation of what you have produced. Tutors should be able to advise on content, but in the nature of things few of them have the time to exercise a real editorial function and even fewer have the necessary experience. But somebody has to do it, if your work is to stand up to the assessor's scrutiny, and not irritate by carelessness and lack of consistency. So, it had better be you! – though it is always desirable that at least one other person should read it before it is submitted; when we read our own writing, we are liable to see what ought to be there, rather than what we have actually written, and so to overlook our misspellings or typing errors. If you can leave time between writing and editing your own work, you have a better chance of seeing it with fresh vision.

A CHECKLIST FOR EDITING

1 Have you explained the objectives of your research?
2 Does the end product fulfil the original terms of reference? Have you done what you undertook to do in the research? If not, have you explained the reason for changes?
3 Do statements made in one place tally with statements on the same topic made in another?
4 Do the interpretations given fit the facts quoted?
5 Do the conclusions follow from the data?
6 Have you given readers enough information to follow and check your reasoning?

Activity	Approximate percentage of time
Structure thoughts	10
Plan product	10
Get relevant information out of store	20
Feed into product plan	25
Write product	35

Table 10.1   Approximate proportions of time required for writing activities.

7 Is the sequence in which information is presented logical?

8 Are terms consistently used and clearly defined?

9 Is the method of presentation appropriate to the purpose and the readership?

10 Is there enough signposting and guidance for readers?

11 Have you provided summaries at the appropriate points?

12 Are recurring elements consistently treated?

13 Is there a text reference to every table and diagram?

14 Has everything been put as briefly as is consistent with clarity?

15 Is the sentence construction logical? (See below for examples of some of the things to watch out for.)

16 Do the chapter titles in the contents list tally with the titles as given at the head of chapters?

17 Is the heading system consistently applied?

18 Is the numbering scheme consistent?

19 Do all the bibliographical references in the text link up with the reference list?

WATCH YOUR LANGUAGE: POINTS TO CHECK SPECIALLY IN EDITING

This book, as you will have observed, isn't about 'how to write good English' in the sense of grammar, syntax, punctuation, etc. I am not sure how much good books of that kind do for those most in need of help. If they have a role, it is as a reference source after writing, rather than as a preparation for doing the job; trying to keep their precepts in mind when in the midst of writing can only be a distraction. But when it comes to editing your own work, it is worth knowing some of the things that professional editors look out for as they do their job, and ways of unspringing some of the traps that writers inadvertently lay for readers. (Whale, 1984, gives useful and far from pedantic advice for those who have to edit their own work.)

Sentence construction

Editors are always alert to the way sentences are put together. Are they properly constructed, or is there a tendency for them not to 'hang together'? These are some of the most frequent ways in which they fall apart – and they mostly do so because the writer is too busy getting the words down to be able at the same time to inspect their relationship to one another:

Singular and plural mixture:

Managers have a tendency to see appraising solely as a means of informing *their subordinates of their weaknesses,* as the time to tell *him* to 'pull *his* socks up'.

The writer has swopped horses in mid-stream from the plural of 'their weaknesses' (which correctly matches 'subordinates'), to the singular of 'him' and 'his' (which doesn't).

Confused construction leading to ambiguity of sense:

The *objective of the workshop was explained* as an attempt to dig further into the obstacles encountered previously *and that the topics were* a vehicle to this end.

This sentence starts with one construction: 'The objective ... was explained as an attempt to dig further into the obstacles', but it ends with another. The second half, which begins 'and that the topics ...' presupposes a different starting construction, along the lines of: 'It was explained that the objective of the workshop was to try to dig ... and that the topics ...'.

Apart from that, the use of 'vehicle' is an odd one in this context; as it was to be used to dig into obstacles, was it some kind of mechanical shovel?

The hanging participle:

One of the easiest ways to create a collapsing sentence structure; most of us do it sometimes. We are led into it by deciding to start a sentence with a phrase beginning with a participle, like 'Having administered the questionnaire'. Nothing wrong with that, but we have to remember that we haven't yet got to the subject of the sentence, and that, when we do, the initial phrase will be read as relating to the person who is the subject (it will have to be a person in this case, because only people can administer questionnaires).

It is, however, all too likely that we shall forget the structural implications of our beginning, and go on with something like this: 'the responses were analysed using a standard statistical package.'

Logically, that construction means that the responses are the subject of the sentence, and that they first administered the questionnaire, and then were analysed. If you find any sentences like that in the course of your editing, you can rescue them by turning them round to get rid of the 'hanging participle' at the start of the sentence: 'When the questionnaire had been administered, the responses were analysed ...'.

Logical but inappropriate structure:
Sentences whose grammatical structure is impeccably logical can still get in the way of understanding. As Kirkman (1980) points out, there is a limit to the number of items of information a reader can absorb in a single unit. Even a reader who is expert in a subject can have difficulty in holding an idea in mind through several clauses until the author finally resolves it. If the ideas are broken down into separate units, so that readers don't have to 'hold their breath', they become not only easier for the expert reader, but also more accessible to the non-expert who does not know the subject and its terminology so well. Klare (1979) uses the idea of 'word depth', or number of 'commitments' a reader must store while reading, to convey the same idea.

This example (written by a journal editor, as it happens, which goes to show that editors are not immune) not only demands a good deal of breath holding, it also embodies some interesting metaphors.

It occurred to me then that for this and for similar subjects [style for articles in scientific journals], we had to have a flag which would join regions and disciplines and not confine our discussions to our inner sanctums nor to this particular detail, though basic and important, but to the myriad of matters where common ground was essential for loosening the clogs in the flow of information and reducing the cost and effort resulting from confusion, redundant effort and fragmentation.

Picture the editors issuing from their inner sanctums to assemble on the common ground, their flag fluttering bravely in the breeze, as they set about loosening their clogs in the flowing stream of information – and you are likely to be so entranced as to forget the serious purpose of the author.

Vocabulary
While structure is the main factor which determines whether readers can easily make the sense that the author intends them to make of the text, the vocabulary used can also influence how difficult they find the task. Kirkman (1980) quotes a survey he con-

ducted among readers who were presented with alternative versions of the same piece of scientific text, which differed among other things in the degree of familiarity and the length of the words used. He found that the weightier and the less familiar the words were, the more difficult did the readers find it to grasp the ideas. He suggests a useful principle, which will stand authors in better stead than an exhortation always to reject long and unfamiliar words in favour of short and familiar ones:

A writer's first obligation is to accuracy of meaning; so when no other word or phrase will express his meaning he must use a long, technical, unfamiliar word – with supporting explanation if necessary. But he should resist the temptation to use long, relatively unfamiliar technical words if there are short familiar words which would convey the meaning adequately.

Active versus passive

'Active verbs are always best' is a generalization which authors should approach with well-informed caution. It is certainly easier to understand instructions if they are in the form 'Now *turn* the dial to the right', with an active verb, than if they are put like this: 'The dial *should now be turned* to the right', with a passive verb. And consistent use of the passive form makes text heavy, and 'neutral' – as if nobody ever did anything, and things were always done by unknown agents. But a blanket rule, 'Throw out all passives', won't do. The passive voice of verbs has a role in life, and writers should understand it. Kirkman (1980) explains it very clearly:

The subject position in a sentence is where we normally place (and look for) the theme or focus of that sentence … By using the passive construction, we move the centre of interest from the 'performer' to the 'undergoer' of the action.

So it is not always in the interests of comprehension to change passive verbs to active ones. Consider this, for example: 'The experimenters in this case kept the residue after combustion for further tests.' compared with 'The residue after combustion was kept for further tests.'

The first version would be appropriate if one were drawing attention to a decision by the experimenters – perhaps it was an innovation they introduced in conducting a series of experiments. The second would be appropriate if the writer were emphasizing that the residue was used for further tests, and that the combustion was not the end of the experimentation.

Punctuation

Logical structure and well-chosen words can still be made mis-
leading to the reader if the writer misuses punctuation – the symbols that should guide the eye and mind to relationships between
structural elements and between individual words. Writers often
find particular difficulty in coming to grips with punctuation.
This is perhaps because we feel the structure of what we say so
strongly within ourselves that it seems impossible that others
should not also feel it. Unfortunately, if there is a possibility of
misunderstanding inherent in the way punctuation is used, *some*
readers are always bound to pick the wrong meaning. It is important, therefore, to be aware of the many pitfalls in this form of
signposting.

Most writers manage to use the full point as a separator
between sentences quite efficiently. Many are too frightened of
the semicolon and the colon to attempt using them. It is, however, worth learning to use them properly; a well-placed semicolon in particular can give neatness and balance to a sentence.
The value of the semicolon lies in its power to link the ideas in
what could be two separate sentences. The linkage gives added
strength and coherence; the semicolon signals to the reader that
what comes after it, while grammatically separate from what goes
before, is conceptually relevant to it.

The colon introduces examples or lists, for instance:

In order to organize information you need:
1 An agreed way of arranging information.
2 A place to store it.
3 Procedures for acquiring information and adding it to the existing stock.

Writers have fewer inhibitions about the comma, and use it as the
all-purpose symbol, sometimes in the right way, sometimes not.
Probably the commonest difficulty is in deciding when commas
are needed to mark off phrases or clauses. Here are two of the
most usual cases:

1 The forms which were used to record interview data were retained for further
analysis after the survey was completed.

There are no commas in this one, and none are needed. The
clause 'which were used to record interview data' specifies which
forms were retained for further analysis. It is essential for meaning that it should be read with 'The forms', and so no separating
commas are required.

2 These forms, which were used to record interview data, were designed by second-year typography students.

In this case, the sentence is indicating a set of forms, and telling us who designed them. The fact that they were forms for recording interview data is incidental to the main information about who designed them, and hence the commas are needed to mark off the clause 'which were used to record interview data' as being a subsidiary piece of information.

Here is a third example, in this case an unacceptable hybrid:

The forms, which were used to record interview data were retained for further analysis after the survey was completed

If a clause has a comma at one end and not at the other, either the single comma must go, or it must have a partner added. Which action should be taken depends on the sense. In this quotation from the *Radio Times,* the missing comma makes all the difference:

The BBC presents a programme about Alfred Hitchcock, who died in August last year with the help of John Russell Taylor and Lindsay Anderson.

Another symbol that causes trouble to writers is the hyphen. Omission is the usual resort of those who are not quite sure, but that is a pity because the hyphen does a useful job in reducing ambiguity. It achieves this by linking two words which can then be added to a third.

Adjective + noun	Compound adjective	Attached to another noun
high + speed	high-speed	high-speed gas
Adjective + participle		
black + headed	black-headed	black-headed gull
Noun + participle		
man + eating	man-eating	man-eating tiger

Sometimes, as in the last example, the omission of the hyphen makes a good deal of difference to the sense.

For some reason, apostrophes have got completely out of hand over the last few years; they turn up where they are not required (especially on greengrocers' blackboards), and go missing where they should be on duty. The apostrophe has two distinct functions:

1 To show ownership:	2 To indicate that letters have been missed out

One owner ['s]

The cat's whiskers

More than one owner [s']

The dogs' dinners

But these words which indicate ownership *never* have an apostrophe:

The cat licked *its* whiskers
The book was *hers*
This house is *ours*
Is that *yours*? No, it must be *theirs*.

can't   cannot
didn't   did not
isn't   is not
it's *   it is

* this is the *only* time that this word needs an apostrophe

References

Donald, M. (1991) *Origins of the Modern Mind*. Cambridge, Massachussetts: Harvard University Press.

Kirkman, J. (1980) *Good Style for Scientific and Engineering Writing*. London: Pitman.

Klare, G. (1979) Writing to inform: making it readable, *Information Design Journal*, 1 (2): 98–106.

Sides, C. H. (1982) Reassessing readability formulas.
In *Proceedings of the 29th International Technical Communication Conference 5–8 May 1982. Boston, Mass*, E-106–E-109.

Shulman, A. D. and Sless, D. (1994) Product labelling regulation. Can it lead to good information design?
In R. Penman, and D. Sless, (eds) *Designing information for people. Proceedings from the symposium*. Canberra, ACT: Communication Research Press.

Whale, J. (1984) *Put it in writing*. London: Dent.

Index